# Personal Selling Strategies for Consultants and Professionals

# Personal Selling Strategies for Consultants and Professionals

## The Perfect Sales Equation

*Richard K. Carlson*

**JOHN WILEY & SONS, INC.**

New York • Chichester • Brisbane • Toronto • Singapore

This text is printed on acid-free paper.

Richard K. Carlson owns the copyright for The "Perfect" Sales Equation.

Copyright © 1993 by John Wiley & Sons, Inc.

All rights reserved. Published simultaneously in Canada.

Reproduction or translation of any part of this work beyond
that permitted by Section 107 or 108 of the 1976 United
States Copyright Act without the permission of the copyright
owner is unlawful. Requests for permission or further
information should be addressed to the Permissions Department,
John Wiley & Sons, Inc., 605 Third Avenue, New York, NY
10158-0012.

This publication is designed to provide accurate and
authoritative information in regard to the subject
matter covered. It is sold with the understanding that
the publisher is not engaged in rendering legal, accounting,
or other professional services. If legal advice or other
expert assistance is required, the services of a competent
professional person should be sought. *From a Declaration
of Principles jointly adopted by a Committee of the
American Bar Association and a Committee of Publishers.*

**Library of Congress Cataloging in Publication Data:**

Carlson, Richard K., 1934–
    Personal selling strategies for consultants and professionals—the
perfect sales equation / Richard K. Carlson.
      p.    cm.
    Includes index.
    ISBN 0-471-59073-8 (alk. paper)
    1. Selling.  2. Consultants—Marketing.  3. Professions—
Marketing.  I. Title.
HF5438.25.C353    1993
001'.068'8—dc20                  93-20089

Printed in the United States of America

10 9 8 7 6 5 4 3 2 1

To Robert T. Brehm

Who gave me so many clues.

# PREFACE

"You don't want to buy a tractor, do you?"

I started my business career developing promotional material for a marketing services agency, and after a couple of years experience, was given the assignment to write a sales training program for a tractor company. Every summer, the company's dealers put on big tent sales with barbecue and corn-on-the-cob and lemonade and they needed to train the dealers' employees on how to sell tractors during these gala events. I was the perfect person to write the program—I had never seen the tractors, never been to a farm implement dealer, and knew nothing about farming. Therefore, experience would not cloud my creative process. I can't remember the name of the company—and it has long since gone out of business. That assignment still haunts me. I can distinctly remember getting the client's approval on my sales approach and wondering, "What if somebody actually tries this?"

This book won't haunt me. I have used every strategy and technique that I write about and have no doubts that if you use them, it will increase your probability of success. Furthermore, reports from those consultants and professionals who have participated in my training programs give me confidence that what works for me works for others as well.

I learned a lot from writing this book. Those of you who have done some training know that you can stand in front of a group and, if you say something with conviction, unless it's outrageous, most people will appear to accept it as true. But, when you take what you have said and put it in writing, the little inconsistencies just leap off the page.

I started this book in December of 1989. I had planned to take the month off and write the book. I didn't finish it in a month, but I got a good start. However, in reviewing what I had written, it became very clear to me that I hadn't really done a thorough job explaining needs, and I treated benefits as if they were something separate from needs. I worked that concept through, tore up almost everything I had written, and developed the Perfect Sales Equation. Although it made a great deal of sense to me, I didn't know if it would help anyone "sell tractors." So, I tested it with the consultants and professionals who attended my course, and I also tested it in my own firm.

My firm, The Carlson/Nathanson Group, Inc., provides consulting for organizational change and training. I have been working with professional firms, consulting with them on how they take their services to the marketplace, and then training them in how to sell those services. In a sense, I'm a consultant's consultant. I also help members of my firm develop their sales strategies. We use the concepts from this book all the time—and we compete successfully against some of the most prestigious consulting firms in the country.

I hope you will try the strategies and techniques discussed in this book. Let me know how they work for you. You can find me in Evanston, Illinois, or Santa Fe, New Mexico. I like to collect consultants' "war stories" . . . especially those with profitable endings.

DICK CARLSON

# ACKNOWLEDGMENTS

To the following people, I offer my thanks.

- If Bill Kenyon, back in the late sixties, hadn't written some guidelines for me, "Doomed is the salesman who . . .", I might not have written this book. I took Bill's 12 points and, over the years, massaged them, added to them, and subtracted from them, and from them began to develop a theory about selling.
- Bob Brehm, to whom this book is dedicated, taught me the value of telling the prospect as little as possible until you really understand your prospect's situation—and then mention only whatever will exactly fit his or her needs. Before working with Bob, I believed that selling was describing your services in your most persuasive manner. Little did I know then that I was ignoring the most important aspects of the Perfect Sales Equation.
- Paul Schneider, a brilliant, thoughtful senior vice president at A.T. Kearney, challenged my thinking, offered contrasting points, and made me feel accountable for what I espoused.

- Jim Gratehouse, whose tutorials on marketing and commentaries on selling stretched my thinking when I needed it most.
- Elaine Filus and Susan Garden helped me a great deal with the manuscript. They proposed order when it was lacking, connections when none were to be found, and suggested, gently, that what may be perfectly clear to me needed a bit more work before others will be struck by my impeccable logic.
- Leslie Nathanson—no contest, the world's best partner.
- Thanks to those who read the manuscript and flattered me with their comments: Sandy Cook, Rick Fumo, Bill Korner, Russ Roberts, Ken Shelton, and Pat Zorsch.
- And to Caroline, whose energy, compassion, and joy of life have dazzled me for three decades.

# CONTENTS

## Appendixes

# 1

# INTRODUCTION

## BOLD PROFESSIONAL INITIATIVES

Professionals and consultants seem to go to great lengths to call *selling* something else: practice development, business development, marketing, or—as the chief executive of a major management consulting firm once phrased it—*bold professional initiatives.* I see nothing wrong with calling it whatever you like—unless your label distorts your understanding of what you must do to get someone to decide to be your client. Regardless of your euphemistic preferences, in this book I will simply call this process *selling.*

On the other hand, *I* don't like the word *selling* either because its stereotype connotes manipulation, or coercion, or some sort of tainted, devious, commercial behavior. Selling some products and services may fit that stereotype, but think of selling professional services as the process of helping a client identify a legitimate, urgent need, and then agreeing upon beneficial solution to that need. No hype, no mirrors, no fast talking.

Selling does not come naturally to many professionals. Although every profession has its share of *rainmakers*—those charismatic, intuitive sellers who attract business in some apparently magical way—most of us do not possess any magic. We have to work hard at selling. And it's easy for us to view selling as a necessary evil that allows us to get paid for providing the services that we were educated to provide.

I did not write this book for the *rainmakers*; I wrote it for those professionals who need a logical sequence of tactics, activities, and techniques to help them gain new clients and develop more business within client organizations.

This book applies most directly to consultants who sell to private industry, but it will also be conceptually useful to other professionals, such as consulting engineers, architects, accountants, software designers. In fact, this book will be helpful to almost anyone who provides an intangible service derived from special knowledge.

## DUMB ADVICE

When I first made a serious attempt at selling, my mentor told me I should look at prospects as "friends I hadn't made yet." That struck me as some of the dumbest advice I had ever received. And 20 years later I still think it's dumb advice. I have never suffered from lack of friends, and the friends I have usually return my phone calls. They seem to understand and welcome my ideas, and occasionally pick up the lunch check.

Therefore, I wasn't sure that I wanted anything to do with selling until I finally convinced myself that selling can be intellectually challenging and can be practiced in a manner compatible with my professional ideals.

## DON'T IMITATE THE RAINMAKERS

I have since developed strategies and techniques to the point where I don't miss many sales—at least the ones that I really work at. I don't consider myself a rainmaker. I do nothing magical. My sales tactics and techniques are all based on theory and practice of the communication process and the dynamics of organizational behavior. So, don't imitate the rainmakers, or try to capture their magic. You'll probably fail, for theirs is an intuitive art. Rather, learn how prospects decide to become your client and then develop sales activities that match those processes.

## HOW THIS BOOK IS ORGANIZED

The first chapter provides a brief overview of the selling process. The next three chapters explore the key concepts driving the activities of that process:

- The "Perfect" Sales Equation,
- Client–consultant relationships, and
- Hierarchy of sales communication media.

After developing those concepts, the book proceeds along two tracks. The first starts when *the prospective client calls you;* the second starts when *you initiate a call on a prospective client.* There are significant differences in the strategies of each track.

The concepts and techniques in this book are intended to increase the **probability** that you will make a sale. Everything that you read here can be challenged situationally with comments that begin with phrases like: "Yeah, but suppose the client . . ." or "If you do that, you're going to . . ." or "Once I ran into a situation where . . ." My only answer is: "Sure, but that's not the way I would bet."

You won't get any scripts for opening conversations, presenting features-advantages-benefits arguments, overcoming objections, or closing the sale. You wouldn't remember such remarks just from reading a book, and wouldn't use the techniques even if you did remember them. However, I will illustrate the points I make with sample dialogues.

## WHAT THIS BOOK WILL GIVE YOU

This book is filled with models, strategies, and concepts that I hope you will interpret and apply. I have tried to make this a realistic book. I have tried to penetrate some of the phrases that roll so easily off a writer's word processor or a trainer's tongue—such as "find the need" and "get to the decision maker" and "build credibility"—and to offer techniques for **actually doing** those things. Such maxims sound easy, but making them happen is hard.

The book is also filled with advice—some of which I have received and I am passing on to you—and some of which I developed after figuring things out, and some I developed after sad experiences. I have learned, for example, that to successfully sell professional services, you need discipline and a positive attitude—technique will follow.

You must have the *discipline* to do something every day that fosters business development or client relationships . . . even when you are overwhelmed with getting the work out the door. You must also have the discipline to do what you know how to do—and not take shortcuts in the sales process.

Attitude? Well, you must first value the services you provide, or you won't insist on your professional standards. And next, you must believe in your fees, or you will sell your services too cheaply.

# 2

# SALES PROCESS OVERVIEW

## DEFINING A CLIENT

I have never been sure what differentiates a client from a customer—probably the term *client* sounds better. One dictionary defines a client as "someone who uses the services of a professional." From a sales perspective, however, I am more interested in defining a *potential* client; that is, someone who:

1. Feels a need.
2. Has the authority to engage the services of a professional.
3. Has the money to pay for the services.

All three qualities must be present: felt need, ability to say "yes," and adequate funds.

## THE SALES PROCESS MODEL

As a professional, you are only a part-time seller and so your sales skills may not have developed to the level of unconscious competence. Besides having to work hard at mastering techniques, you will need a framework, or model, to remind you of the scope of the sales process. The model will help you determine where you stand with a given prospect and will enable you to plan your next step.

The diagram of the Sales Process Model shown in Figure 2.1 has three sections: Initial Opportunity, Add-On Opportunities and Follow-On Opportunities.

### Initial Opportunity

The Initial Opportunity emerges from the first contact, whether by a prospect or a seller. The figure indicates the distance between the initial interview and submitting a proposal. I can't tell you how many calls should fill that space, but you should never submit a proposal until you've done a thorough job of selling.

### Add-On Opportunities

During discussions with your prospective clients, you will likely discover facts or information suggesting you can sell something in addition to the services discussed in your initial opportunity. Add-on Opportunities should not be ignored, nor should you automatically include them in your primary proposal. More on that later.

### Follow-On Opportunities

The most effective business developers sell the next engagement before they complete the current one, and are always looking for follow-on opportunities. You may have heard the myth that claims follow-on business is much easier to get than the first job. It may be easier, but not much. In fact, to be successful in selling follow-on business, you must apply just as

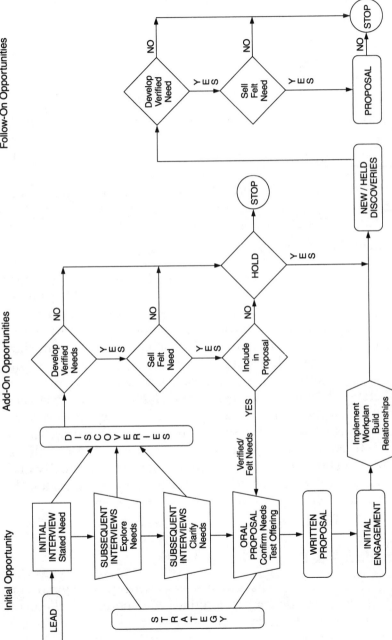

**Figure 2.1 The Business Development Process Model** (Copyright 1990 by Richard K. Carlson. All rights reserved.)

7

much strategy and energy, despite the advantages of knowing the players and of working from a position of established trust.

## CRITICAL TIME FACTORS

Selling intangible services takes longer than selling tangible products because the buyer must make at least two decisions:

1. Does the solution presented by this professional meet my needs?
2. Do I want to work with this professional on a one-to-one basis?

### In Search of a Quick Hit

The model may seem overly complicated, and following it may seem to demand more time than you have available. That's natural: Most sellers want the quick hit. And most likely once or twice in your career, you will make a fantastic "one-call close." Be sure, however, you recognize that such successes are an aberration. The one-call close does not necessarily mean that you did everything right, it means you mostly got lucky.

Sellers almost always feel a greater sense of urgency than buyers. Consultants, in particular, tend to show little patience with prolonged sales processes. You have other things to do. Since you cannot devote the majority of your time to selling, you look for shortcuts. Those shortcuts, however, can really hurt you. To increase your probability of success, you must match the pace of your sales activity to the pace of your prospect's decision-making process.

### Intangibles—A Description and a Promise

Other issues prolong the process of selling professional services. Because you sell an intangible, your potential client receives only a verbal description of your service and a promise that it will produce the desired outcome, on time and within budget. If you put yourself in the potential client's position, you will recognize that decisions requiring such a high degree of trust are seldom made quickly.

## More Delays

Some potential clients, initially, may have only a vague idea of their needs. In that situation, you must spend time clarifying needs before you can offer an acceptable solution. Clarification involves gaining mutual understanding and agreement. Even architects, engineers, and commercial interior designers, who can depict their offerings graphically, must patiently engage in the lengthy process of gaining client understanding and agreement. Most other professionals must rely on verbal descriptions—frequently full of jargon or technical terms—to describe services and to build customers' trust.

## One Size Does Not Fit All

Professional services are inherently customized. You don't sell a "one-size-fits-all" product (except when your client convinces you that you sell a commodity and forces you into a price-sensitive, look-alike offering). Custom services require time-consuming, front-end analysis and iterative discussions.

Respect your client's need to scrutinize your service and deliverables, and respect the time required for effective communication. You possess special knowledge. You may have spent years accumulating it, and you use it every day. What may be very simple and logical to you may be very difficult for your client to understand.

Unskilled sellers, encountering frustrating delays, frequently panic into submitting a premature proposal, which inevitably is off target. Then, they blame their failure on "stupid clients who don't really know what they want."

## CREATING A COMPETITIVE ADVANTAGE

Think through your sales strategy just as carefully as you would think through an engagement work plan. Use exactly the same skills in selling that you use in consulting: good communication and good understanding of the client's situation and environment. There is nothing magical in this formula. Keep in mind that effective selling takes time, and your willingness to invest time can create an immense competitive advantage.

# 3

# THE "PERFECT" SALES EQUATION

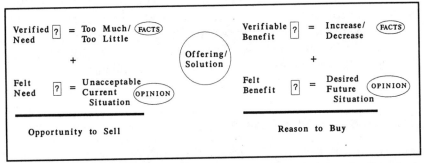

**Figure 3.1  The Perfect Sales Equation** (Copyright 1992 by Richard K. Carlson. All rights reserved.)

An Equation? No, it's not really an equation, nor is it perfect. The Perfect Sales Equation (PSE) is a metaphor and a model that can be critical to preparing a sales strategy and to evaluating your progress. This model should be the foundation for everything you do.

I have used the equation metaphor because a well-designed sales proposition should perfectly match up the values of the needs with the values of the benefits. Although a perfect match may not be possible, it's a goal worth working toward.

## SOLVING FOR THE UNKNOWNS

In this equation (see Figure 3.1), you try to solve for four unknowns before you design your offering: (1) Verified Need, (2) Felt Need, (3) Verifiable Benefit, and (4) Felt Benefit.

### Verified Needs and Verifiable Benefits

The Verified Need(s) must be documented by facts, that is, a condition within the client organization indicating too much of something or too little of something. Examples might be: too much time in the distribution system, too few prospects converted to customers, too much cost in a product line. And, because the flip side of a need is a benefit, the Verifiable Benefit(s) must also project facts—something that will be increased or decreased. A quick example: A consulting engineering firm is successful in one out of five proposals for major contracts. A Verifiable Benefit would be to improve that ratio to one out of three.

### Felt Needs and Felt Benefits

Felt Needs and Benefits are formed by opinions; that is, the decision maker and key influencers agree that too much or too little of something has created an *unacceptable* current situation, and that increasing or decreasing something will create a *desired* future situation.

To continue with the preceding example, closing only one out of five proposals does not become a Felt Need until those with responsibility declare that the situation is unacceptable. And, the benefit won't be felt until those with responsibility say that closing one out of three is what they want. For the decision makers to say, "Yeah, we're not happy with our proposal-to-close ratio, and we'd like to get that lots lower" is not a strong enough statement of purpose to be called a Felt Need or a Felt Benefit.

In Figure 3.1, Verified Needs *plus* Felt Needs produce the *opportunity to sell* something. Take away one or the other, and the opportunity is either diminished or gone. Similarly, Verifiable Benefits *plus* Felt Benefits give prospects a *reason to buy*. Failure to help prospects perceive both types of benefits weakens their reason to buy.

## Solution and Offering

The solution to the prospect's needs, which is described in the offering that you propose, is something that will turn Verified Needs into Verifiable Benefits, that is, it will transform the current unacceptable situation into the desired future situation.

## TEMPTATIONS THAT LEAD TO FAILURE

Many sellers behave as though they believe that a good idea will sell itself. They shortcut the confirmation of the Verified and Felt needs and ignore the benefits completely because, they say, the needs and benefits should be "all too obvious" to the intelligent buyer. Occasionally, someone will make a quick sale with this approach, if the prospect likes the offering and if the prospect has the unilateral authority to make the buying decision. But that's not the way to bet.

Another problem is that consultants—who may begin a sales interview by asking questions intended to uncover needs—often become sidetracked. As soon as the prospect mentions something for which they have a solution, they snap at the bait and begin describing what they can do, usually in terms of "Here's what we've done in situations similar to yours." Not only do these consultants present a solution prematurely, but they deter the prospect from telling them more about the needs.

For the presentation of a solution to result in quick sale, the prospect must *instantaneously* perceive both the needs and the benefits that make the idea valuable. If the prospect cannot *instantaneously* perceive the needs and benefits, the idea serves only as an entertaining topic for a brief conversation. Most often, that conversation will end with the prospect saying something like, "That's a really interesting idea. It may have lots of merit. Let me bounce it off some people and I'll get back to you." That, friends, is a euphemism for "no sale."

### Case History

Some two years ago, two consultants from the communications practice of a leading benefits and compensation consulting firm met with departmental decision makers in a client organization, a major, multinational corporation. The consultants' main objective was to give a demonstration of their voice response system (VRS). A VRS allows employees to get information about their company savings, retirement, and health care plans by calling a telephone number, keying in their employee identification number, and selecting items from a menu. The client did not have a voice response system, and because it considered itself a "leading edge" company, the consultants thought it would be a good prospect for purchasing their system.

After giving a comprehensive demonstration of the system, the consultants reported, "They [the client decision makers] were interested, but nothing ever came of it." Now, two years later, the consultants have decided, "We are ready to sell VRS again. Because of the recent enhancements to the system, we think there might be more opportunity now." So, they have arranged another product demonstration. The question you should consider is, "Is another demonstration an appropriate strategy?"

What are the chances of making the sale? In my estimate—pretty slim. And if they do make the sale, the reason won't be their selling expertise. Rather, it will happen because the conditions at the client organization have become more favorable for considering a VRS system. Perhaps the client has available money in the budget, and the system now seems like a good idea. So, in reality, corporate circumstances, not sales strategy, will have created the sale.

You can analyze the consultants' likely failure by looking again at Figure 3.1. The consultants' focused their sales efforts on demonstrating what they had to offer (their VRS product). The planned to put on a slick and professional demonstration that again described the system's enhanced features, suggested some benefits, and compared it with other competitive systems. There is no indication that the sellers spent any time trying to verify the need, such as that departmental personnel were spending too much time answering standard questions or giving out standard information (Verified Need). We have no evidence that the decision makers felt that the amount of time being spent was unacceptable (Felt Need). There is also nothing to show that the department heads understood how much time the VRS would save (Verifiable Benefit), or that they realized employees could make valuable use of the captured time (Felt Benefit).

If the consultants had approached the sales opportunity with data—either real or good guesses—about the amount of time department personnel spend providing standard answers and standard information and about the amount of time the VRS could save, then they could have used the meeting first to determine whether the department *felt* the need and felt the benefit. And then, if the department heads had responded positively, the demonstration would have proved that their system could resolve the need and produce the benefit.

In terms of the Perfect Sales Equation, the ideal case—such as the one just described—allows you to solve both unknowns in the need side of the equation: You will be able to develop powerful and irrefutable data verifying that the need exists and causes the client to feel a great deal of urgency for getting the need resolved. You also will be able to solve both unknowns in the benefit side: You and your client will agree on what constitutes success and how to measure it, and the client organization will be satisfied with the projected level of success for your solution. Seldom, however, do things work out quite that well. You may solve some of the unknowns "perfectly," but others will remain partially or completely unsolved. *Any part of the equation that remains partially or completely unsolved represents a vulnerability in your sales strategy.*

Before going further, reality-test this model. Think about a sale you didn't expect to lose, or better still, think about a sale that you are currently pursuing. Ask yourself some tough questions:

- Has my prospect accepted (as complete, accurate, and relevant) the data that indicate too much or too little of something?
- Has the decision maker said that those data represent an unacceptable situation?
- Have you and the decision maker reached agreement about what the future should look like . . . the degree to which something should be increased or decreased?
- Have all the people who can influence the buying decision agreed with your description of the desired future situation?

Chances are, you'll find some vulnerabilities in your equation. The bad news is that you have some more work to do. The good news is that you know exactly what you have to do.

## VARIATIONS ON NEEDS

We'll explore three variations: the Presumed Need, the Expressed Need, and the Requirement.

### Presumed Need

As a professional, you are highly skilled in discovering needs for which you can provide solutions. As you research a prospect or as you work with a client, you will probably get information indicating a need. The need may be obvious to you, but not at all apparent to anyone else. And it's not because your prospect is stupid, shortsighted, or unaware. There are many reasons you may see something that your prospect does not:

1. You are trained to find needs.
2. You get paid for fulfilling needs, so you have a major interest in finding them.
3. You can concentrate on where to look.
4. You are seeing the need for the first time, and your client may have already decided it's a low priority or unfixable.

*When you presume a need exists, you must develop the verified and felt need side of the equation before you can sell something.*

### Case History

An investment banking firm sells its products through securities dealers. The company has had an unbroken string of record years in sales and profits, even in those years when much of the investment community experienced difficult times. While doing some other work for the firm, you discovered that about a third of its sales force of approximately 100 representatives turns over in the first year of employment. Your experience tells you that the turnover rate is far too high.

You found out that the regional managers, who do most of the recruiting, hiring, and initial training, spend as much as 25 percent of their time on those activities. You talked with each regional manager, and all agreed that the turnover rate is unacceptable. They feel that they could better spend their time in managing sales. At this point, you feel extremely optimistic that your Presumed Need may lead to an engagement where you could study the causes of turnover and then propose some solutions. The decision maker, you have found out, is the Vice President-Marketing.

When you meet with the VP-Marketing, however, he tells you that because of the nature of the firm's compensation system and the type of employee who "feels at home" in the company the turnover rate is neither unexpected nor undesirable.

By applying the Perfect Sales Equation to the above case, you can easily verify your Presumed Need as well as the Felt

Need of *some* key people in the organization. Unfortunately, the decision maker doesn't feel the need. In other circumstances, your best strategy would be to develop the consequences of the turnover so that the VP could recognize the problem. In this case, you might be able to do that, but it would take a lot of time and ingenuity. And you can probably find a better place to invest your time—at least until your prospect's string of record sales and profits breaks.

## Expressed Need

A prospect, when calling you, may use the term *need* to describe the *absence of a solution*. For example, the prospect may say something like, "We need to find someone to help us write a strategic plan and mission statement." If you're in the business of writing strategic plans and missions statements, you might be tempted to propose an engagement. Before you do so, however, remember that a strategic plan and a mission statement are solutions to something, and at this point, you don't know anything about the needs. What does the company have too little or too much of? The answer is *not* that the company lacks a strategic plan or a mission statement, or that it has no one capable of writing the plan and the statement. The need is that the company's employees have too little understanding of the firm's strategic direction, overall purpose, and values. The Expressed Need(s)—a strategic plan and a mission statement—are not needs at all, but, rather, the prospective client's opinion of what may be appropriate solutions.

Consultants faced with an Expressed Need must decide whether the prospect has correctly analyzed the situation and prescribed the right solution. If you agree with a prospect's prescribed solution, then the Expressed Need becomes a Requirement. A simple example of this would be prospects who say they need financial audits—certified financial statements. It doesn't make any sense to explore for the underlying needs; the prospects want to buy audits, and that's what they are going to buy, either from you or from someone else. On the other hand, sometimes you must look more deeply into a prospect's Expressed Need.

Case History

A gourmet chocolate manufacturing firm, a subsidiary of a large, diversified conglomerate, has three major profit centers: (1) national sales, through department stores; (2) retail sales, through company-owned stores; and (3) mail order, through corporate and consumer gift catalogs.

You meet with the manager of the mail-order operation who tells you of the extraordinary recent growth in her area. She complains that the data-processing (DP) fulfillment services provided by the parent company's mail-order division no longer have adequate capacity for her needs, and that this deficiency created serious problems during the previous holiday rush period. Furthermore, the mail-order data processing must be corrected before the next Christmas season. She asks if you could propose setting up her own data-processing capability.

Let's analyze this selling situation using the Perfect Sales Equation. The prospect's Expressed Need was for her own DP capability. Should you view this as a Requirement? Probably not—the initial discussion does not indicate that the manager has carefully analyzed the situation before concluding that developing her own DP capability is the best of several possible solutions. This seems more likely to be a fishing expedition; the prospect might use your proposal as a free feasibility study to learn what it would take to develop her own DP capability. So, before starting to write a proposal for a DP study, see what you can learn by applying the PSE.

Is the Verified Need that the parent company's mail order division has too little capacity to serve this manager's needs? Maybe, but maybe not. It's worth your time to look deeper into the situation to find the real need. (You might also wonder whether you should get paid for analyzing this situation, or whether you should make an investment, hoping it will lead to a real assignment. That question will be covered in a later chapter.) Where do you start? You could begin by analyzing the current system. Or, better still, you could explore the business function being affected—in this case, the fulfillment function. The real need, if it exists, could be:

- Too many orders were fulfilled at such a late date that they were not delivered in time for Christmas.
- Too many orders received within "X" number of days before Christmas could not be fulfilled, and the orders were refused.

So the data to look for to verify the need are the number of orders delivered late and the number of orders refused because they could not be delivered on time. Once you have collected those data, you can then ask your prospect, "Do these data represent an unacceptable current situation?" To which she will probably answer, "Of course they do! What did I already tell you? I need by own DP capability!"

Possibly, your prospect is right; she doesn't require all your data if she has sole decision-making authority to buy the new system and the funds to pay for it. But she probably doesn't. It is unlikely that she is senior enough in the organization to make independent buying decisions. Therefore, the data you have collected will become extremely useful in:

1. Determining if developing independent DP capacity is the best solution.
2. Selling your solution to the people who do have the ability to buy.

So, armed with the data, you can move to the benefit side of the equation and ask the manager what she wants. Does she want zero orders delivered late and no orders refused if received before, say, December 22nd? When she declares the Verifiable Benefit and says that's what she is willing to pay for (Felt Benefit), then you can look for the possible solutions. And, what are they?

One answer could be to provide separate DP capabilities, another could be to expand or alter the current parent company capabilities. Still another could be to take some time out of the order-processing system. At this point, who knows what is the better alternative? But, what you do know is that if you had written a proposal for identifying her DP needs and presented a hardware and software recommendation, your prospect would have thanked you profusely, complimented you on your thorough and timely response, and promised to get back to you in a week or so. Two weeks later, not having heard from her, you would call. She would apologize for not getting back to you and explain that she has run into some corporate roadblocks but still hopes to go ahead with your proposal. Keep in touch.

## Second-Order Needs

When you accept the prospect's solution, that becomes the prescribed deliverable, the Requirement. For example, if your prospect has said that he wants your proposal on a treasury operations review, that service is a Requirement of your offering. Now you face the most difficult selling challenge of all: differentiating your offering from the competition, which also will be proposing a treasury operations review. You can differentiate, however, by using the PSE to focus on second-order needs, that is, the work-process needs or service needs associated with the delivery of the Requirement.

**Work-Process Needs.** These needs relate to how the work gets done, such as special cost-cutting software (for the client who needs to save money); qualitative interviews rather than questionnaires, or some other industry expertise that allows you to produce the work in less time (for the client who needs to save time); or some project management system that immediately documents change orders or overruns (for the client who needs continual reassurance).

Most consultants never even think about connecting their approach to a project with what the client needs. Yet, in a competitive sales situation between well-qualified firms, your work plan or process capabilities can become the focus of the buying decision.

## SERVICE NEEDS

Service needs are another factor that may differentiate you from your competition. For example, public accounting firms, when requested to propose on an audit, will typically write a proposal that includes service claims in hopes that these extras will give them a competitive advantage. It's easy to spot these claims since they appear as last-ditch efforts to persuade the prospect that "an audit is not an audit is not an audit." Furthermore, almost every proposal includes the same claims: "Continual partner involvement," "Responsive to your needs," "Effective flow of communication." In addition to providing boring reading, these claims probably suggest no value to the prospective client unless the seller is lucky enough to hit on a true service need that can be verified and felt.

In competitive sales situations, spend some time discussing service with your prospect before you write your proposal. Ask questions such as: "Tell me about how you worked with XYZ firm in the past. What was their service like? And, what can we do to improve on it?" You may learn that the incumbent audit firm seldom sent out a partner for client meetings, or usually delivered the tax returns right up against deadlines. Now, you may have found service needs that you can respond to, presuming you have verified them with data and have found a key player who says the current level of service is unacceptable. The verified service needs in this case might be defined as (1) partner attends only the opening and closing meetings, and (2) the most recent four returns were completed within two days of deadline. Your next step, then, is to work with your prospect to determine how often a partner *should* attend meetings and when tax returns *should* be completed. That information can be included as part of your proposal.

Second order needs can be subtle, but if you can find and develop them, you just may create a competitive advantage.

## TAKE A BREAK

The "Perfect" Sales Equation is the most important concept in this book. You now should have a good grasp of it . . . however, certainly, some aspects require further explanation. But, before going on, take a break, let the concept sink in. Then, go on reading. When you're back, we'll take a look at some of the common difficulties you will experience when you apply the "Perfect" Sales Equation.

## IDENTIFYING A VERIFIED NEED

Some business developers have difficulty analyzing the selling situation deeply enough to discover the *fundamental* Verified Need. Often this is because prospective clients won't allow access to such important information, but usually it's because the consultant hasn't asked the right questions or probed the answers deeply enough.

To illustrate getting at the fundamental Verified Need, let's explore the simple and useful example of excessive turnover in a company or department. If a prospective client says, "We need a program to reduce turnover," you could say that the need was the absence of a program to reduce turnover. The "too much/too little" criteria for the Verified Need can be interpreted to fit; having no program is certainly "too little." It's OK to stay at that level of need if the client has turned the stated need into a Requirement. However, if the client has *not* turned that need into a Requirement, you must look more deeply to discover the Verified Need.

The next level of need is the turnover rate itself, say, 25 percent per year. You could state that the Verified Need is *too much* turnover in the department, and if every member of the Buying Center[1] agrees—meaning that they all express a Felt Need—then you can sell to that level of Verified Need. However, if some members of the Buying Center *disagree*—they do *not* feel that 25 percent turnover is too much— then you have to look to a deeper level to verify the need. You will find that deeper level of need when you explore the *consequences* of the high turnover rate. That is, you must look at the business functions affected by the high turnover rate.

---

[1] All those who can influence the decision to buy a service or select a service provider. Chapter 10 discusses the Buying Center in detail.

In an earlier example, I mentioned an investment banking firm that experienced a turnover of about a third of its sales force each year. Senior management did not *feel* the need to reduce turnover because their selling was transaction-based rather than relationship-based and because customers did not complain about the "revolving door" of sales representatives. The turnover didn't seem to affect the company's sales. What's more there was an excellent supply of bright, energetic job candidates who were eager to work for the firm. If their selling had been relationship based, the fundamental verified need probably would be that *too many* customers are complaining about the lack of continuity with their sales representative.

## GETTING A FELT NEED CONSENSUS

A Felt Need is highly subjective because it is derived from opinions about two criteria: *urgency* and *importance.* Members of the Buying Center who believe both these factors are present will say that the Verified Need describes an *unacceptable current situation,* whereas dissenting members may think the current situation is important but not urgent, urgent but not important, or neither. Therefore, they do not have a Felt Need. When you detect dissension among the Buying Center, first try to identify the reasons some members do not have a Felt Need. Then, to establish urgency and importance so that these members will change their opinions, look for different ways to interpret or present data that verifies the need. For example, a consultant who looked into office efficiency at a large law firm reported the Verified Need as inefficient procedures that "cause a great deal of unnecessary effort for the administrative staff." The firm's partners, listening to this report, expressed interest in the problem but were not moved to fund a redesign of their office systems. However, when the consultant later translated the inefficiencies into delayed billing, unbilled reimbursable expenses, and a surplus of administrative staff, the partners felt the need immediately.

## FINDING APPROPRIATE SOLUTIONS

Once you have verified the needs and the Buying Center has agreed that the current situation is unacceptable (felt need), you'll be tempted to develop and present your solution. Before doing so, however, you'll find it pays off to look at the benefits side of the equation, and determine whether your solution will, in fact, provide a benefit to all parties involved.

Complex organizations have many competing self-interests, so the solution that produces a benefit for one group may, in fact, create a problem for another. For example, in some organizations, high turnover in one department may be a problem, but reduced turnover may not be the appropriate solution. To illustrate, the internal auditing department of a money center bank by default became a recruiting ground for other bank departments, causing extremely high turnover among second- and third-year auditors. The internal auditing department did such a good job recruiting bright, motivated people whose capabilities were showcased during the audit process that other departments pirated their best and brightest. Obviously, the high turnover rate presented a problem to the audit department management. On the other hand, reducing the turnover rate did not serve the best interests of the bank or the young auditors, who wanted career mobility. Therefore, a program designed to prevent young auditors from leaving the department was not an appropriate solution. However, a program that *managed* the turnover rate presented a more attractive alternative. In this case, the Verified Need was that the internal auditing department had too much *unscheduled* turnover among its better young auditors. This Verified Need suggests a far different solution than a program that would reduce the departmental turnover rate.

## IMPORTANCE OF THE VERIFIABLE BENEFIT

Consultants often have difficulty with this element in the Equation. Some professionals argue that they are prohibited from guaranteeing specific results such as cost savings. This provides a good rationalization for not talking benefits at all. The real reason, however, may be that not clarifying the benefits seems to allow some room to maneuver in the engagement. This space may look highly desirable from the consultant's viewpoint, but it's illusory at best.

The Verifiable Benefit, in defining what the desired future situation should look like, becomes the flip side of the Verified Need. It is important in two ways:

1.  It helps decision makers make the buying decision.
2.  It helps build client satisfaction. If you and your client agree on what constitutes a successful project, chances are you'll both be satisfied—and client satisfaction builds long-term relationships.

First, let's look how it helps decision makers buy.

When a large Buying Center or a task force discusses a potential project, someone who is not totally in favor of the plan will usually say, "How are we really going to know if we've fixed anything and if we have gotten our money's worth?" This question indicates that some members of the Buying Center have not identified the Verifiable Benefit or don't agree on its value. Unfortunately, you may not be in the room when that question is asked. Unless someone has an answer, that question can stall the decision-making process, or worse, kill the project. Now, let's look at how poorly defined benefits can affect a profitable, long-term relationship.

A consultant who avoids this element of the equation puts the client relationship in jeopardy because the client's expectations may exceed what the consultant planned to deliver. Some desired future situations are easily verifiable, such as expected (not guaranteed) cost reductions and expected (not guaranteed) increases in productivity, because the measurement devices are conventional and already in place. Other Verifiable Benefits, however, require new measuring devices that can be extremely difficult or expensive to create or employ. For example, some organizational development engagements may have some highly abstract and difficult-to-measure benefits. The outcomes of some training programs may be virtually impossible to measure because skill acquisition does not guarantee on-the-job performance. Keep in mind, however, that regardless of the difficulty in specifying outcomes, your offering and your relationship are vulnerable to the extent that this element of the equation remains unclear.

## GETTING A FELT BENEFIT CONSENSUS

Like Felt Needs, the Felt Benefit is derived subjectively from opinions. At its simplest level, the Felt Benefit is consensus among the Buying Center members that the benefit would produce *their interpretation* of the desired future state. Clearly, members can easily disagree, although such disagreements are often merely misunderstandings that can be mediated without much difficulty. On the other hand, when the decision makers represent a variety of interests, getting agreement on the Felt Benefit can be difficult. Individual members of the Buying Center will tend to evaluate the expected benefit in terms of personal costs.

Putting a monetary cost (probably the price of the service) on the benefit is usually easy and so is quantifying the cost of the need. If the cost of the benefit is less than the cost of the need, it should produce a done deal. Sometimes, however, nonmonetary costs can get in the way. For example, the office systems study mentioned earlier may conclude that the law firm can reduce its administrative staff. But when it does that, it will sacrifice its ability to deal with overload conditions. If a few of the partners live by crisis, the staff reduction could affect them severely. Or the staff reduction may require terminating a loyal employee. Because it hurts to fire such an employee, that action can be defined as a cost—to the one who has to do the firing. And there is at least one more cost: If the law firm accepts the consultant's recommendation, the partners will have to learn to use a new, automated system—the cost being that they must give up the security of the familiar system.

Therefore, when you cannot get the members of the Buying Center to agree on the Felt Benefits, you must try to discover what your solution causes each member to *give up*. In searching for these costs, consider such high-value intangibles as status, privacy, and the comfort of established routines.

## APPLYING THE PERFECT SALES EQUATION

You can begin the sales process at any place in the equation: by discussing needs, suggesting benefits, or describing an idea—an offering or expected solution. I recommend starting where your prospect wants to start. But no matter where you begin, you haven't finished until you have tried to solve each unknown in the equation.

The Perfect Sales Equation will serve as a "pulse-check" to tell you at any given time what you have accomplished and what you still need to do. And as you prepare your final presentation or proposal, it will help you develop a strategy that emphasizes the strengths of your offering.

# 4

# CLIENT–CONSULTANT RELATIONSHIPS

## THE SECOND KEY CONCEPT IN SELLING

The Perfect Sales Equation appeals to many professionals because of its underlying logic and its analytical value. But, to the dismay of many technically oriented consultants, selling is more than logic and analysis: It's two or more people deciding to exchange values. Underlaying every prospect's buying decision is the question: "Do I want to work with this person?"

Part of the answer to that question depends on interpersonal factors, chemistry, or rapport—good fortune when it happens, bad luck when it doesn't. The more controllable part, however, pertains to the professional relationship between you and your prospective client. As the seller, you can choose how to characterize that relationship. But before making a decision, you should determine the kind of relationship envisioned by your prospect.

## View from Across the Desk

Buyers may anticipate major risks when they hire a professional to perform a service. In addition to significant fee payments, these risks can involve ego, stature in the organization, and in some instances, careers. As you go about the process of selling, your prospects will evaluate what kind of risk you pose both to the company and to themselves.

In the course of your sales calls, your prospects' questions, the degree to which they are willing to answer your questions, and their level of enthusiasm often indicate the amount of risk the project poses for them. Try to pick up these signals of perceived risk from prospects:

- Do they feel threatened that you may have more competence or knowledge in special areas?
- Do they resent your working conditions and compensation?
- Do they suspect that you may be difficult to control?
- Are they afraid you will pass judgment on their abilities and accomplishments?
- Are they worried that you may discover and disclose additional problems?
- Are they concerned that your recommendations may reduce their authority, responsibilities, or career opportunities?
- Are they doubtful that you will deliver what they have contracted for?
- Are they uneasy that your recommendations may turn out to be impractical?

If you have the sensitivity to detect some of these risks, you can try to resolve them through your interpersonal skills. However, sometimes a buyer will send out extremely subtle signals that you can easily miss. So, if you don't feel skilled in detecting interpersonal subtleties (and I don't), you can use another approach.

## CONSULTANT ROLES

You can try to figure out which of the following roles the prospective client expects you to play:

1. Trusted business advisor, or partner.
2. Expert.
3. Implementer.

### Trusted Business Advisor

Certainly, you would like all your clients to think of you as their "trusted business advisor." What an ideal situation, from your point of view. In that kind of relationship, your clients feel dependent on you. They call you with every problem that involves your area of expertise, and when you suggest some project, they usually accept your recommendation. They don't keep you on edge by soliciting or entertaining conversations with your competitors. And they don't pressure you to discount your fees.

Some professional services lend themselves to a trusted business advisor relationship and some don't, the difference being the likelihood of high-frequency contact. For example, law firms and advertising agencies may have opportunities to develop such relationships because of the *continuity* of their work. Other professionals with episodic services, however, do not get sufficient "face time" to develop a trusted business advisor relationship.

A trusted business advisor relationship cannot be sold. If it can develop at all, it will evolve over time. However, some client organizations prefer an arm's length relationship with their consultants because they perceive conflicting interests regarding dependency. Whereas professionals want to cultivate their clients' dependency, clients may feel threatened by dependency. Consultants want a full-service relationship; clients, however, often want to retain the option to buy the "right service at the right time."

Clients' *inability to measure the quality of professional services* can be another reason for not wanting to become dependent on a single professional services firm. Think of it this way: If a manufacturer buys raw materials, it can test those materials to determine their quality. If it buys a piece of machinery, it can test its output data or its run life. But, how do clients measure the quality of the professional services they purchase? How do clients know they are getting the best available, or all that they pay for? They must either trust the provider or create an environment that keeps such professionals "on their toes."

Some clients find an easy solution by spreading their business among competitive firms or by threatening to entertain competitive proposals. Others become difficult clients— challenging your recommendations and invoices. Some clients fear that if professionals get too comfortable, the quality of their services may decrease while their prices increase.

## Expert

While the trusted business advisor relationship may be ideal, don't be disappointed if you have to settle for an "expert" relationship. In this role, your clients ask you to analyze situations and to make recommendations. They value your opinions and give you access to others within the client organization who can help you come up with the most appropriate solution. You get to exercise your professionalism.

## Implementer

I doubt that you want to be perceived as just an implementer, which means that your client defines both the need and the solution, and then asks for your proposal on implementing the solution. Clients seeking only implementation usually will invite several other proposals. It is rare to be a sole source proposer in an implementer relationship.

Because this relationship is constraining—both professionally and economically—you should try to change the relationship to that of expert. You can do this, but it's not easy. First of all, clients who feel many of the risks mentioned at the beginning of this chapter do not want an expert relationship; an implementer relationship seems much safer. Furthermore, some clients may not want an expert because they already have one: themselves. Therefore, you must find some need/benefit to change the relationship, and you can do this by applying the Perfect Sales Equation. If prospects believe that the current state (with the client as the expert, and you as the implementer) is the desired state, there is no need. To get clients to value you as an expert, you must either show that their approach (current state) is inadequate (undesired) or that you offer an approach (future state) that is superior (desired).

I recommend showing clients what you can offer and trying to convince them that your approach is more desirable. I've never had much luck getting clients to view me as a savior after I have made them feel inadequate.

## Suggested Strategy for Change: Implementer to Expert

Before you "bounce your idea" off your prospect and expect him or her to recognize immediately its superiority, spend at least a little time developing your persuasion strategy. The following elements should go into the strategy; the order in which you present them will depend on the situation:

1. Demonstrate, and get agreement, that you understand your prospect's approach.
2. Confirm the objectives, including requirements, specifications, and criteria, that any approach must satisfy.
3. Discuss the pros and cons of your prospect's approach.
4. Present your approach; highlight why you think it better satisfies objectives.
5. Discuss your approach.

Another application of this strategy, to change or expand the scope of the proposed assignment, will be discussed in Chapter 12.

## MAINTAINING AND IMPROVING
## YOUR RELATIONSHIP

Most consultants have heard that the best source of new business is their existing clients. It's true. Consequently, you can expect sizable dividends from the time you invest in maintaining relationships. The operative word is *invest*, which means you devote time and resources toward keeping the relationship viable.

The following list outlines some excellent investment strategies suggested by David H. Maister, a consultant who specializes in advising professional firms:[1]

*Making the Client Disposed to Use Firm Again*

1. *Going the Extra Mile on the Current Engagement*
   Use new business budget to fund extra analysis.
   Use budget to improve turnaround time, service.
   Improve quality of presentations.
   Offer more documentation, explanations, accessibility.

2. *Increasing the Amount of Client Contact*
   Telephone regularly.
   Visit at every opportunity.
   Schedule business meeting near mealtime.
   Invite to firm offices.
   Introduce one's partners.
   Get firm leaders involved.

---

[1]Maister, David H. 1989. "Marketing to Existing Clients." *Journal of Management Consulting*, 5 (2).

3. *Building the Business Relationship*
   Help the client with contacts.
   Put on special seminars for the client's staff.
   Volunteer to attend client's internal meetings.
   Offer free day of counseling on nonproject matters.
   Send the client useful articles.
   If possible, refer business to the client.

4. *Building the Personal Relationship*
   Engage in social activities.
   Remember personal, family anniversaries.
   Obtain scarce tickets.
   Provide home telephone number.
   Offer use of firm's facilities.

### Case History

A few years ago, we hired a woman for our organizational behavior practice who had no experience as an outside consultant. Our first clue that she would become an outstanding business developer came at the time she told us she had decided to come with us rather than accept the position of Director, Human Resources, for the capital markets division of a large international bank. She said that when she turned down its offer, she had told the other firm that she could do the management development audit (which was to have been her first assignment) equally well as an outside consultant. The firm's management bought the idea, and she had sold her first job before her first day on our staff. At full rates, too.

After completing the job, she came to me and asked what she should do next. Because I had recently read Maister's article, I said something like, "Call them at least every month, take them to lunch at least every three months, and send them articles and ideas that you think would be useful to them." With a beginner's unquestioning innocence, she did all three things extraordinarily well, and she has brought in an almost continuous stream of noncompetitive projects from that client for the past three years, many of which she has initiated. Her role with that client has evolved from implementer to expert.

## HAVE YOU HUGGED YOUR CONSULTANT TODAY?

I doubt that we'll ever see such a bumper sticker, because professional/consulting relationships are usually so tenuous. There are legions of stories about clients who have been "burned" by consultants or who have been subjected to arrogant professionals. Although many of the horror stories are true, you occasionally hear stories of consultants who have made wonderful contributions to their clients' businesses. Possibly the best way to begin and maintain good client relationships is to learn from Arthur Andersen & Co., whose stated purpose is "to help our clients succeed." That credo sounds simplistic at first, but it implies that clients ultimately define what their own success should be, and also define the role consultants should play in helping to achieve that success.

# 5

# THE HIERARCHY OF SALES COMMUNICATION MEDIA

In the Introduction, I referred to three key concepts that are critical to understanding and eventually mastering the sales process. You have explored the first two: the Perfect Sales Equation and Client–Consultant Relationships. That brings you to the third, the mildly academic-sounding "Hierarchy of Sales Communication Media,"[1] or more simply put, selecting the right medium to communicate a specific message at a specific time.

Let me offer a few generalizations, just to get your attention:

- When prospects ask if you could send some literature before they agree to an interview, say "no," nicely (and don't say that you would rather drop it by, either).

---

[1]This chapter is largely influenced by the article, "The Selection of Communication Media as an Executive Skill," by Robert H. Lengel and Richard L. Daft, *The Academy of Management EXECUTIVE* (1988), II(3): 225–232.

- When clients ask you to make a presentation because they would like to "run your ideas by a couple of key people," say "no," courteously.
- When your boss says that this proposal "has got to knock their socks off," tell him or her that it "can't be done," respectfully.

## THEORETICAL CONSTRUCT

Many salespeople would never get past this subheading because, to them, theory is anathema. You, too, may be hesitant because the term *theoretical construct* implies "heavy" reading, and in general, that is not a popular pastime these days. But, being a professional, you are probably comfortable with the written word and skilled at abstracting theories into practical application. However, don't expect your client to like to read just because you do. I have found the theory of the hierarchy of sales communication media extraordinarily useful. By helping me rethink some of my communication practices, it has saved me from killing at least one sale and another major relationship.

### Intuitively Understood

What follows is not startling information; most professionals know that one medium, in a given situation, works more effectively than another. Regardless of what people may *know*, however, I frequently observe them *using* the wrong medium because it's more convenient or avoids confrontation, or "that's the way we've always done it," or they think they must respond to a letter with a letter. So, this model will serve as a reminder to turn your knowledge into application.

## RICH AND LEAN SALES MEDIA

You can segregate sales communication media into two types: rich and lean. The richest sales communication medium is the one-on-one, face-to-face conversation. The leanest one is a brochure. Let's identify the characteristics of rich media and contrast them with lean media. Then, we'll explore their appropriate uses.

## Rich Media Characteristics

In one-on-one communication, you increase the *probability* of receiving immediate and meaningful feedback. Immediate feedback is that which occurs during the conservation, not sometime thereafter. Meaningful feedback provides clear, direct evidence of whether your prospect understands or misunderstands what you have said, and agrees or disagrees with it. Grunts, smiles, nods, and silence may be immediate, but not meaningful.

Rich media have personal characteristics—in focus and in effect. A personal *focus* means that you can shape your message exclusively to the person receiving it, which allows you to be relevant (listeners quickly stop listening to messages they decide are irrelevant). A personal *effect* means that rich media—because of personal contact—can help build relationships.

Communication theorists say that a rich medium is multicued, meaning it uses more than words to convey meaning. It adds inflection and nonverbal components to enhance understanding.

A rich medium, such as face-to-face communication, increases the probability of a more controlled environment. Both parties probably pay attention to each other's messages, and distractions can be minimized. A rich medium in itself gives a message special importance. Simply choosing to communicate one-on-one makes your message seem significant.

## Comparison of Rich and Lean Media

Now, let's compare rich and lean media by considering the characteristics of a brochure. Does a brochure provoke immediate and meaningful feedback? No, not likely. Is it personal in focus and effect? No. It is designed for a mass audience, and it contributes little if anything toward building a relationship.

Is a brochure multicued? Yes, if, in addition to words, it uses charts, graphs, and photographs to aid understanding. Is the brochure's message delivered in a controlled environment? Absolutely not. It must compete for attention with everything else in the prospect's in-basket, and everything else on his or her calendar.

Lastly, does the lean medium of a brochure convey a sense of importance? No. Recipients can easily defer or ignore such a message. So, what value does a brochure provide in the sales process? Well, it lets a prospect know you can afford to have a brochure printed. But, it certainly won't sell anything for you, and it can work against you, as you will read about in Chapter 8.

## Uses of Rich and Lean Media

Conceptually, you should use rich media to communicate ambiguous, nonroutine messages and lean media for documentation and retention. When selling, therefore, use the richest media at your disposal because your messages certainly are ambiguous

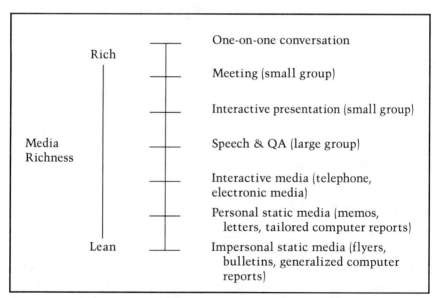

**Figure 5.1   Media Richness Hierarchy** (Adapted from Robert H. Lengel and Richard L. Daft, "The Selection of Communication Media as an Executive Skill," The Academy of Management EXECUTIVE, 1988.)

and nonroutine. Then, use lean media to record and confirm what your client has bought.

Figure 5.1 evaluates the common sales communication media in terms of richness and leanness.

## PRESENTATIONS

Many sellers believe a presentation to a small group of key influencers and decision makers provides a great opportunity to sell. It may appear efficient, in the sense that the presentation pulls together all the important people in the same place and at the same time. Furthermore, group dynamics can, in fact, produce a positive, consensus-building effect. As you will see later, however, if you make your presentation with the intention of *selling*[2] the group something, chances are you'll fail. When possible, use the small group presentation to *confirm* what you have *sold* one-on-one because any group presentation is less rich than one-on-one conversation. Let's test the richness of a small group presentation.

### Feedback: Immediate and Meaningful?

Some people feel inhibited in a group, and won't speak up. Small groups are political bodies, and candor suffers. People will say things one-on-one that they won't say in a group. And, people will say things in a group that they won't say one-on-one. Some people will attack your message, posturing for their bosses and colleagues. Groups tend to defer decisions, and you frequently get conclusions such as, "Thanks for your time. That was an informative presentation. You gave us a lot to think about . . . and now we need to do *our* homework. So, give us a week or so to think this over and we'll get back to you." This is hardly meaningful feedback.

---

[2]An exception is the "short-list" presentation, typically required in competitive sales situations. This is discussed in Appendix A.

## Personal?

A small group presentation cannot be exclusively personal because everyone in attendance has different interests that affect how they understand, distort, or ignore your message. Prospects are selective and rather poor listeners in a group setting.

## Controlled Environment?

Sometimes, people arrive late; sometimes, they leave early; and sometimes, a key person never shows up at all. Group members may have side conversations or arguments or look through handouts while you are speaking. Participants may exercise hidden agenda, or go off on tangents. And, occasionally, someone may fall asleep.

## Implied Importance?

Yes. In fact, a presentation may imply more importance than you want. Presentations are seen as a major statement and, therefore, tend to encourage "go–no go" judgments or invite "devil's advocate" criticism. If you fail to make a strong positive impact during your presentation, you may have ended your sales opportunity.

## Purposes for Small Group Presentations

That's another subject—and maybe another book. The short answer is that, ideally, you should use small group presentations to convey information or to confirm a sale. However, you will occasionally get trapped into making a small group presentation for the purpose of selling. In that situation, exercise the time-honored activity of "greasing the skids." Meet with key people ahead of time. Test out your ideas and arguments. Find out what opposition you can expect. And, most importantly, try to sell, one-on-one, those key people before they ever enter your presentation room. You can argue that one-on-ones consume a lot of time, but so does trying to resell an idea that has once been rejected.

## PROPOSALS

Although a proposal is often thought of as a major sales tool, in most cases, a great proposal cannot overcome a poor job of selling, but a bad proposal can damage a good job of selling (see Chapter 14 for additional information about proposals). A proposal is your final statement, and it prompts an accept/reject decision. You may get feedback, but it is usually too late to do anything with it.

Is the content personal? It all depends on the ratio of boilerplate to client-specific content. And, it depends on the sequence of the content. Any proposal that begins with "An overview of our firm" or "Our firm's capabilities to meet your needs" does not suggest that a highly personalized message will follow. Any proposal that begins with a couple of paragraphs describing the client firm ("AJAX is a $135 million manufacturer of electrical equipment for the home construction industry based in Chicago, Illinois") does not impress your prospective client that you understand the firm, it means that you can read and copy a Dun & Bradstreet report.

Most proposals that I have seen do not employ multiple cues. Very few have charts and graphs. Seldom are they reproduced in color. And, the writing is anything but colorful. Reading most professional service proposals is slightly more fun than reading an insurance policy. What's more, most of the phrases in professional service proposals are competitively interchangeable. All consultants say they "are responsive to client needs," "offer full-service capabilities," "are dedicated to quality," and ensure "active partner involvement." Consequently, these phrases have no meaning.

Convey importance? I would like to think that those people who receive proposals actually read them. But at best, they usually thumb through them, zeroing in on the price section. Or, some member of the selection committee is delegated to create a selection matrix and to abstract from the proposal information to put on the matrix. That saves the selection committee a lot of time.

Studies have shown that reading habits and capabilities in the United States have declined significantly. Experience has taught me not to count on anyone reading any sales communication that exceeds one page. So, does it make sense to produce a 30- or 40-page proposal? In most cases—architects and engineers excepted—no. In fact, the very bulk of the proposal may inhibit someone from reading it, rationalizing, "I can't take the time to look at this now, I'll get to it tonight." Don't take bets on that probability.

## New Age Proposals

Recently, I have looked at some proposals that astound me. A major benefits and compensation consulting firm produced the most elaborate proposal I have ever seen. Its client, Microsoft, a Fortune 500 company, distributed a Request for Proposal (RFP) for a "study and potential implementation to a full flexible benefits program." The lead to the RFP stated hypothetically:

Dateline: January 15, 1994

Cover of *Fortune* Magazine

"Employee Benefits . . .
The cutting edge of the 21st Century is available today
at
MICROSOFT"

Not surprisingly, this lead and the evaluation criteria in the RFP almost guaranteed that "show biz" proposals would follow. The RFP stated:

Proposals and presentations will be evaluated based on the following criteria:
- Creativity.
- Presentation of "fair playing field."
- Responsiveness and quality of submission and presentation.

- Past experience and ability to perform work of a similar nature.
- Technical abilities to achieve the scope of the work.

## Big Bucks Proposals

The resulting proposal from the incumbent was an expensively produced, simulated *Fortune* magazine and informational supplement. The "magazine" was a first-class production, 24 pages, complete with full-color cover, original photography and artwork, and articles that described the proposed program and highlighted the past accomplishments of the incumbent firm.

Is this the New Age of proposals where staid professional firms will start looking like advertising agencies? Why would Microsoft list "creativity" and "responsiveness and quality of submission and presentation" so prominently in its evaluation criteria? Does it mean that buyers of professional services are so bored by commonplace proposals with irrelevant boilerplate and stilted writing that they'll try anything to get more interesting submissions? I hope that our professional capabilities will not be judged by show biz standards, but I agree that most professional service proposals are more soporific than stimulating. I think it makes sense to try to make professional proposals more interesting. The following anonymous quotation, however, suggests a good balance between cleverness and substance: "Cleverness is serviceable for everything, sufficient for nothing."[3]

As the selling of consulting services becomes more competitive, and as differentiating competitors becomes more subjective, elaborate and creative proposals are likely to become more common. The downside of that approach is that the cost of proposals will increase and jobs may be awarded for the wrong reasons. If indeed this is the trend, I find it disturbing. I think you will feel the same way if you read Neil Postman's *Amusing Ourselves to Death*.[4] It's hard to stop the creep of show biz once it gets started.

---

[3]Fortune cookie, Bangkok House, Chicago, 1992.
[4]Postman, Neil. 1985. *Amusing Ourselves to Death*. New York: Viking Penguin.

## MORE LEAN MEDIA

### Telephone

This medium seems rich, but performs lean. The telephone is an intrusive medium. Count on people being engaged in some other activity when your phone call comes through. The first decision they make when their telephone rings is, Do I listen to this message or do I fake it? Chances are, you'll never know which decision they make. Therefore, restrict your use of the telephone to extremely brief messages.

### Useless Letters and Memo Wars

A useless letter is any letter written to sell an idea or solve a problem—the subject matter is, obviously, controversial. As a good rule of thumb, if you have something controversial to say, do it in person. Consultants frequently defend their decisions to write a controversial letter by saying, "I wanted to be very careful to use just the right words." There are a couple things wrong with that reasoning. First "specific language" is an oxymoron; what may be "just the right words" for you may be misconstrued by the reader. Second, when you're involved in a controversial matter, you need feedback on your message to clarify meaning.

If your client sends you a memo complaining about some aspect of performance or some billing issue, do not respond with a memo. Although it is extraordinarily tempting to fire back your response, don't do it. Get together and discuss the issue, even if it takes time you don't have and even if you think you can clear things up with a written note. Memo wars are little skirmishes that escalate into broken relationships.

## EXIGENCIES

Circumstances often make it impractical to use the best medium. Therefore, use media combinations to enhance the probability that you will communicate effectively. For example, call someone to tell the person you are sending a letter that you'd like to discuss later on the phone. The first phone call improves the probability that your letter will be read, the second gives you feedback on what was understood and agreed.

Use the telephone to schedule a telephone conversation. If you can't be there in person, call your client and say, for example, that you need to talk over budget figures. Specify that it will take about 15 minutes and that he or she will need to refer to the last status report. Then ask when it will be a good time to talk.

It's difficult to believe that people don't listen carefully to your telephone messages because you know that you have important things to say. However, if you doubt that people pay poor attention to telephone conversations, think about your own telephone habits. How often do you sort through mail while on the phone, continue looking at a report while talking, or take a phone call in the middle of a meeting?

## ILLUSION

Market research pioneer Pierre Martineau was quoted as saying, "The great enemy of communication is the *illusion* of it." Martineau has taught us that if we believe we have communicated and have not, our subsequent actions will probably be nonproductive. Whenever we use the wrong medium for an important message, in all likelihood, we have created that dangerous illusion.

# 6

# SALES TALK AND COMMUNICATION STYLE

**Consultant:** (Smiles broadly; looks prospect squarely in the eye with an air of confidence) Mr. Prospect, what specifically are your goals in improving the effectiveness of your department?

**Mr. Prospect:** It's really very simple. Our inventory costs have been rising rapidly, and we're looking for ways to get them back under control. I thought you could suggest some answers.

**Consultant:** Let me see if I understand you correctly. You want to lower your expenses and tighten up your operations. Is that it?

**Mr. Prospect:** That's about right.

**Consultant:** Lowering costs is certainly important, Mr. Prospect. If I could show you a good way to do this, would you be interested?

**Mr. Prospect:** I guess so.

**Consultant:** Of course you would. Our Mark III inventory control system would be an excellent choice for your company. It costs 20 percent less to buy and use. That means you'll save money right away and throughout the year. How does that sound, Mr. Prospect?

**Mr. Prospect:** Well, I'm not sure . . .

**Consultant:** I see you have a concern, Mr. Prospect. What's troubling you about what I've said?

**Mr. Prospect:** Well . . .

The preceding lines, with only minor changes, are from the beginning of Calman Phillips' article "The Not-so-Sweet Sound of Sales Talk."[1] Phillips is the first person I know of who has challenged what many authorities on selling skills recommend as the way that business developers should talk. Referring to his dialogue, he writes, "This is not the way real people talk when they discuss problems, present solutions or reach joint decisions." So, why should sellers be trained in such dialogue?

Because I agree with Phillips, this book will not contain useless recommendations for the exact language to use when asking questions, overcoming objections, or closing a sale. Although some of the following chapters contain sample dialogue, its only purpose is to show how a technique plays out—and I hope the dialogue sounds real, not like "sales talk."

## USING QUESTIONS

Questions are your most important sales communication tool. As a professional, you should already have skills that enable you to gather from others the facts and opinions needed to explore a subject thoroughly. And, while you use exactly the same skills in the process of selling, you probably do not use them as effectively in

---

[1]Calman P. Phillips, *Training Magazine*, September 1988.

that context as you do in the consulting context. The reason for this lies in the purpose of your questions.

While consulting, your sole purpose for questioning is investigative; in selling, your goal is to uncover a need that your service might fill. Therefore, in selling, you will direct your questions toward those areas that you think may contain some hint of a need. What you hear your prospect say will also be biased by *what you want to hear*, that is, by your desire to find a need you can fulfill.

## LANGUAGE DIFFICULTIES

Regardless of the affability of the conversation and your apparent rapport with a prospect, the prospect knows you have something to sell and that you want to persuade him or her to buy. Consequently, there is a natural tension between the two: the prospect's cautious management of information versus your attempts to ferret out needs. To compound this problem, language will get in your way.

Education has given you and your prospect the ability to speak fluently in abstract and metaphoric language. Together, you can talk about "being competitive" and "lean and mean" and "empowerment" and "price sensitivity" and "productivity," feeling comfortable that you at least share a common jargon. But, that's the problem. You can share the language, but you probably don't share the meaning because the abstract terms you use preclude a common definition. Unfortunately, *we think we understand each other because we use the same words fluently.*

### Helpful Techniques

Practitioners of general semantics addressed this communication barrier years ago, and lately, proponents of neurolinguistic programming have repackaged the same concepts.[2] These

---

[2]Readers of Peter Senge's *The Fifth Discipline* (New York: Doubleday Currency, 1990) will also find these concepts related.

approaches can help you cut through the fog of language by showing you how to break down or "unpack" abstract nouns and verbs, in other words, to apply "critical thinking." For example, your prospect tells you, "We're going through a major restructuring." The abstract verb is *going through* and the abstract noun is *restructuring.* At this point, you have a general picture of what is happening, but you don't know what specific change process going through means, nor do you know anything about their restructuring. But, if you want to find a need for your services, you must find out.

## That's Obvious!

My guess is that four out of five of you readers believe that you already have the skills to spot abstractions and clarify them. But I would like you to consider this perspective: that while you may understand the concept of critical thinking intellectually and may do it well in the process of your consulting or professional fact-finding, I doubt that very many of you actually apply critical thinking during sales conversations. Consider this possibility.

## To Build Rapport You've Got to Sell Yourself!

During a sales call, you work very hard to build rapport. You try to encourage your prospect to like you. You show that you both speak the same language and that you agree on the same concepts. You try to demonstrate that you are very bright and can understand everything your prospect tells you. Unfortunately, this overriding desire to build rapport and to sell yourself can stop you from applying critical thinking to your prospect's statements. You're too busy being nice and making friends. However, the following two techniques will be helpful in such situations.

1. *Indefinite Nouns.* When you hear a noun that sounds indefinite, ask, "What, specifically?" For example, your prospect

may say, "We've just got to get more competitive by the end of the year." You can then say, "I'm interested in understanding what specifically you are shooting for when you say *more competitive.*"

2. *Indefinite Verbs.* When you hear a verb that sounds indefinite, ask, "How, specifically?" For example, if your prospect says, "Right now, we're exploring all possibilities," you can ask, "Could you tell me, specifically, how you are doing that?"

## Apply Reasonably

You may have correctly concluded that much of the language we use is to some extent abstract. So, if you apply critical thinking to everything your prospect says, you'll cover very little ground and probably drive your prospect up the wall. Therefore use the technique judiciously. Take notes of what your prospect says, copying verbatim what sounds to be the most important abstract words or phrases you hear. Put an asterisk after these terms. Then, when your prospect has reached the end of a topic, refer back to the terms requiring clarification. For example, "As you were describing the conditions here at the plant, you used the term *hostility* a couple of times. How do the people actually show hostility, and what seems to be causing this hostility?"

Prospects often use abstract terms when describing who will be involved in the buying decision and how the decision will be made. A prospect once told me he only needed to "run it [my proposal] by" the executive vice president, and I assumed from what he said and the way he said it, that this action was merely a courtesy. Later, I found out that the EVP was the decision maker. When you hear people described as "major players" or "out of the loop," it is easy to accept these abstractions without clarification, only to find out later that you didn't really understand enough about these individuals and their roles in the decision-making process to allow you to develop a successful sales strategy.

## Two-Value Orientation

In addition to clarifying abstract language, be aware of the problems in two-value orientation, the academic term for *either/or* polar comparisons. Scholars have pointed out that the English language is rich with words that describe extremes, such as hot/cold, rich/poor, now/never, profit/loss, for/against, go/no-go, short-term/long-term. The Japanese language contains far fewer polar words, and many words and phrases that describe the gray areas between the extremes. Therefore, they are conditioned to discuss gray areas to ensure everyone understands. Such differences have caused some scholars to speculate that the nature of our language influences how we reach decisions. No one will argue that the Japanese, for the past three decades, have made many good business decisions. Could one of the reasons be that they have avoided two-value, either/or thinking?

Clearly, you must question your prospect when you hear a two-value orientation. If your prospective client says "Right now, we're looking at either turning this department around or outsourcing the whole thing," you have just struck a mother lode of abstract language and two-value orientation. It is an invitation, not just to clarify language, but to discover some real business opportunities. "How are you looking at it? What are you comparing? Who's helping you? What other options have you considered? Who will be affected by your decision? How will you know if you've made the right decision? How important is this situation?" The answers to these clarifying questions could lead to an attractive engagement.

## What Causes Objections?

Objections grow from disagreement, misunderstanding, or a little of both. Dr. Kenneth Johnson, a leading communication scholar, has written: "We must expect to be misunderstood. We must expect to misunderstand."[3] In my opinion, most objections are based on misunderstanding, not complete disagreement. As a

---

    [3]Johnson, Kenneth G. 1972. *General Semantics: An Outline Survey.* San Francisco: International Society for General Semantics.

seller, that's the way to bet, and the way to approach resolving an objection.

## Best Advice

Every book on negotiation or persuasion will give you this same advice: "Clarify an objection before you refute it." And, while the advice may be impeccable, it's almost against the laws of nature, at least, a salesperson's nature. A typical salesperson hears an objection and immediately unleashes his or her best argument. You, however, don't want to be a salesperson; you want to be a professional who sells. Therefore, you should not rise to the same bait that attracts the typical salesperson. Practice this concept every chance you get, both in social and in business situations, so that you can eventually internalize it: *Clarify the objection before you refute it.*

## COMMUNICATION STYLE

The current literature on selling contains many references to using prospects' communication style or social style to identify and understand their buying motives. Presumably, you can then organize your sales message to appeal to prospects' buying motives, they will buy. I think that using style stereotypes to pinpoint buying *motives* is a bit of a stretch. People and organizational buying decisions are far more complex than would be implied by that concept. Nevertheless, understanding your own communication style, and the style of those with whom you communicate, can be extraordinarily important in building interpersonal relations and in preparing yourself for a buyer's predicted behavior. Part of a buyer's decision is, "Do I want to work with this person?" If your communication style conflicts with that of the buyer, the answer could be "no."

## Style Instrumentation

You can find quite a few instruments on the market that measure or purport to measure social or communication style. Most instruments are either self-report or other-report. *Self-report* means that you complete the survey about yourself; *other-report* means that you select other people to describe your behavior. Based on evidence our firm has compiled over the years, self-report instruments can be excellent for identifying your *values* but are not adequate for describing how you *behave.* Our approach[4] includes a self-report and five other-reports. Our data indicate that in roughly 50 percent of the cases, the self-reports do not agree with the other-reports, indicating that many of our "focal individuals" do not see themselves as others see them. Since both instruments have extremely high statistical validity and reliability, I have concluded that a great many people are quite poor at observing their own behavior.

## Style Nomenclature

Most instruments use a two-axis, four-quadrant model and are based on similar concepts. In our instrument, the horizontal axis measures the extent to which you use Dominant communication behavior; the other axis measures the extent to which you use Open communication behavior. The names we apply to our quadrants are: Controlling Style, Analyzing Style, Facilitating Style, and Advocating Style. If you are familiar with other nomenclature, such as driver, expressive, sensor, and intuitor, you can easily translate.

The following are *stereotypical* behaviors associated with each style.

| **Controlling Style** | **Analyzing Style** |
|---|---|
| goal-oriented | process-oriented |
| disciplined | precise |
| organized | thorough |
| efficient | inquisitive |
| pragmatic | prudent |

---

[4]The "Perceptive Communications" training program and "The Communication Style Survey" are copyrighted properties of Intracom, Inc., an affiliate of The Carlson/Nathanson Group, Inc.

**Controlling Style**

determined
directional
independent
competitive

**Analyzing Style**

stabilizing
logical
patient
correct

**Advocating Style**

idea-oriented
creative
enthusiastic
expressive
stimulating
energetic
spontaneous
intuitive
talker

**Facilitating Style**

people-oriented
loyal
team player
accepting
cooperative
friendly
empathetic
supportive
listener

The style concepts are valuable in adapting your communication behavior to avoid conflict with the style of the person with whom you are communicating. For example, when I meet a prospect for the first time, I try to discern whether the prospect's style is more or less dominant than mine. If I sense that the person is more dominant, I try to speak with greater conviction, I leave out small talk, and I get down to business quickly. If the prospect is less dominant, I slow down and prepare myself to talk about subjects of his or her interest. This may sound simplistic, but if I have only one opportunity to start a relationship, I don't want to bore or waste the time of a prospect who is more dominant than I am, and I don't want to push someone too hard who is less dominant. A mistake either way could end up being a reason not to select me for the work.

If the person is more open than I am, I assume that the prospect would like to establish a personal relationship. I can detect openness by the amount and type of information the prospect discloses. If the person is less open, I assume that he or she does not want a personal relationship with me—yet—and is not going to tell me much until I have established a greater sense of trust.

The style concepts prove equally valuable in predicting how a buyer might behave during the decision-making process. The following lists suggest predictable buyer behavior by style.

**Selling to the *Controlling* Style.** Expect these prospects to:

- Provide you with good direction on how to structure your offering and how to sell it within their organization; will want your credentials but probably will not check them.
- Show impatience while you explain concepts to provide background information; therefore, stick to pragmatic issues.
- Not be interested in your proposal until "the time is right," which probably means a competitive situation.
- Then, ask for your proposal "tomorrow," complete with a breakdown of costs; they will want a price before you've had a chance to do a thorough study; they will be impressed by quick response.
- Try to reduce the elements of competitive proposals to a single point of comparison—price; therefore, try to quantify "value."
- Regard the diagnostic or research phase of a project as a discrete project, with no obligation to proceed to the next step; therefore, try to sell Step 2 while working on Step 1.
- Not see the need for you to interview others in the organization; therefore, you must be prepared to make a strong case.
- Challenge your price; challenge your time frame.
- Test you with objections.
- Not spend much time reading premeeting or follow-up materials; therefore, cover all important information directly and briefly.
- Make decisions quickly and firmly; if decisions are delayed, ask for the reason.

**Selling to the *Facilitating* Style.** Expect these prospects to:

- Be willing to spend time with you—and probably to exaggerate both the likelihood of doing business together and the perceived value of your services; therefore, qualify the prospect before investing substantial time.

- Want to establish personal rapport before discussing business, requiring that you invest time in the relationship.
- Encourage you to present or propose your ideas even if the project is not firm.
- Avoid criticizing your ideas—even constructively; therefore, you should emphatically request critical feedback.
- Be ineffective in selling a controversial idea within the organization; have difficulty defending ideas against criticism.
- Continue to profess an interest in your proposal, but avoid making a commitment.
- Take time making decisions, and to need deadlines.
- Be sensitive to organizational politics, and to exaggerate their complexity.
- Want to meet your "project team" and to have your team tour their facilities.
- Form a personal attachment to the person most instrumental in leading the sale.
- Be overly concerned with the interests of all members of the Buying Center and how your proposal affects them.

**Selling to the *Advocating* Style.**    Expect these prospects to:

- Be easy to see, but not to pay much attention unless your project suggests an immediate benefit.
- During an interview, they may open up and get excited before you have completed what you need to cover; therefore, recognize that they probably have been thinking about their concepts rather than your information.
- Remember only the low end of your ball park or range price estimate.
- Try to convince you to lower your price because of the "great, future opportunities" for you after you have successfully completed this engagement.

- Underestimate potential project problems, especially availability of funds and information.
- Dominate meetings and explore interesting tangents; therefore, be prepared to use power tactfully or humorously to keep them on track.
- Make decisions quickly and easily, but subject to change.
- Want to sell your idea internally without your help; therefore, spend time ensuring that they really understand the needs, the solutions, and the benefits.
- Overestimate their own influence, authority, and autonomy.
- Work with you in bursts, possibly sidetracked by other interests.
- See the big picture when discussing your services; therefore, communicate with metaphors, analogies, and anecdotes.

**Selling to the *Analyzing* Style.**   Expect these prospects to:

- Prefer to begin the relationship with written communication, and later, scheduled meetings.
- Be difficult to see unless there is a defined project.
- Have less interest in establishing personal rapport than in establishing a professional relationship.
- During the initial interview, describe the situation and need, but not divulge personal interests in the project.
- Ask questions of you that have purposes beyond information gathering; therefore, do not leave the subject until you have found out the purpose for the question and the evaluation of your answer.
- Describe the project as complex; therefore, ask many questions to demonstrate you understand its complexity.
- React unfavorably if you provide a quick solution; therefore, delay offering a solution and provide alternatives from which to choose.
- Read your proposal carefully, noting discrepancies, inconsistencies, and "typos."

- Be interested in the experts you can bring to the project; will not hesitate to consult their own experts.
- Require exact figures, not rough estimates.
- Make a deliberate, thoughtful decision.

## PERSONAL RELATIONSHIPS

Selling a consulting or professional service requires building a strong relationship with the buyer. But that doesn't mean that you have to become the buyer's buddy. Age, gender, and personality differences often make that improbable. You often hear complaints of consultant behavior related to differences in style.

| Label | Style Difference |
|---|---|
| Arrogant | Too much dominance |
| Academic | Too little dominance |
| Superficial | Too much openness |
| Unresponsive | Too little openness |

To pick up the signals indicating that your style and your prospect's style differ significantly, simply let your prospect talk. A colleague told me years ago that you can judge the quality of a sales call by the amount of time your prospect talks—the more the better. If you can avoid monopolizing the conversation, you will accrue many benefits: You'll gather important information, you'll avoid sales talk, and you'll pick up on the prospect's communication style, so that when you do open your mouth, smart things will come out.

# 7

# INITIAL CONTACT: WHEN THE PROSPECT CALLS YOU

Your marketing efforts and reputation pay off when a prospect calls you, either through a referral or a direct request. Another possible initial contact, the request for proposal (RFP), requires a different approach, and so it is covered in Appendix A.

## CALL PREPARATION—ESTABLISHING COMPETENCE

Much of the literature on selling recommends extensive precall preparation. While I cannot present an argument against extensive precall preparation, from my observation, people seldom do it. Therefore, I see little value in recommending something that you'll probably not do, so let's look at the amount of preparation that seems realistic.

As a general guideline, the less experience you have, the more preparation you need. In this initial call, the prospective client may make a decision either to continue discussing the project with you or to reject you immediately as a candidate for the project. The prospect will use three criteria to make that decision:

1. Are you competent? That is, do you have sufficient knowledge and experience, and have you made an effort to understand my organization and my needs?
2. Are you credible? Do you speak with enough confidence and substance that I believe you can develop and implement a successful solution?
3. Do I want to work with you?

Obviously, prospects cannot make a well-reasoned decision about your competency, credibility, or compatibility on your first meeting. But, they will make a decision anyway, using what they believe are valid *indicators* of those qualities. For example, if you have taken the time to learn something about the prospect organization and its business, and if you are prepared to *ask insightful questions*, you will have provided good indicators of competency. This is fairly simple to accomplish by learning what is public knowledge:

- Basic products and market niche.
- Size and structure of organization.
- Basic financials, and whether they are trending upward or downward.
- Anything newsworthy in past six months.

Make a list of the questions you plan to ask and write them out in the language you would use in front of your prospect. You need this list because you probably will experience some stress during the interview that will affect your recall and composure. The list will enable you to:

1. Remember to ask all the important questions.
2. Concentrate on your prospect's answer and avoid worry about thinking up your next question.

3. Phrase your questions in an open-ended format, such as: "What seems to be . . . ?" or "Under what circumstances does this usually occur?"

4. Impress your prospect that you came prepared: "I wrote out some questions that I wanted to be sure to ask you . . ."

Many professionals think that relying on a list of questions gives the impression that you need a crutch. Nonsense. What's more, I'm willing to bet that you will never hear a prospect say to you, "I'd like to do business with you, but I noticed that you had to write out some of the questions that you asked, so I've decided to go with your competitor."

Whereas the extent to which you have *prepared* for the call will affect your perceived competency, the way you *conduct* the call indicates your level of credibility and what it would be like to work with you.

## CREDIBILITY

The prospect, in addition to making some decision about your competence, will decide about your credibility—that is, whether you can do what you say you can do. Credibility seems to tie in with *enthusiasm* and *conviction*. There is a difference between enthusiasm and conviction. Both are important, and both can be dangerous. Being too enthusiastic suggests superficiality, and having too much conviction suggests a closed mind. But, then again, who wants to do business with someone who shows neither enthusiasm for the assignment nor the conviction of being able to produce a successful solution? The following list suggests techniques for hitting the appropriate level of enthusiasm and conviction:

- Avoid hyperbole, such as "I know you want to do business with the best, and we are going to deliver the best."
- Avoid claims, such as "We have unquestionably the top research analysts in the business."

- Avoid equivocation, such as "Well, that really depends on so many factors that I wouldn't want to offer an opinion at this time."

## COMPATIBILITY

The prospect may think you are competent and credible, but does the prospect really want to work with you? Best case for the buyer is to hire a consultant whom he or she really enjoys being with, who will become a close friend. Next best is for the buyer to hire a consultant who is easy to work with. You can't always create the best case, but by paying attention to your potential client, you can figure out ways to work well together. At this point, we will focus on creating the impression of compatibility.

In the preceding chapter, you learned how Communication Styles can affect compatibility. But, there is more to it than style. You begin to develop compatibility, that is, a business-based, interpersonal relationship, (1) by *listening*, (2) by giving direct answers, and (3) by giving the prospect something of value. Don't worry about finding something in common, such as hobbies or special interests, you already have enough in common: The prospect has a need, and you think you can resolve it. That's good enough for now.

### Listening

Since listening is an internal activity, nobody can tell for sure whether you are listening or daydreaming. In fact, some people listen very carefully even though they don't look as though they are. To build a compatible relationship, you not only have to listen, but you have to *look* as if you are listening. That means, maintain eye contact, sit erectly, take notes, and then ask questions of clarification and expansion.

## Giving Direct Answers

Consultants often avoid direct answers, for good reason. They are generally careful and thoughtful because they understand that seldom is something as simple as it seems at first. Nevertheless, prospects need direct answers—not necessarily *final* answers. For example, the prospect asks, "How would you go about putting a value on a company?" The consultant, not a business valuation expert, answers: "Well, it depends on a lot of factors. What I'd like to do is get you together with one of our business valuation experts. I think you'll find that . . ." In a better scenario, the consultant should be prepared to answer: "In general, there are three things that we would look at: your market value, your assets value, and your equity in those assets. But, it's much more complex than that. So, rather than gathering a lot of information that I would have to feed back to our valuation expert, I'd like the three of us to get together."

Prospects frequently ask my partner, Leslie Nathanson, how much a cultural change project costs and how long it will take. She answers, "Twice . . . twice as much and twice as long as you could ever imagine it would." Then, she goes on to give her prospect some range prices and time estimates. Prospects need to have some idea what they are getting into, what the path toward the outcome will be, and what costs they must face.

## Giving Something of Value

The third part of creating compatibility is to give your prospects something of value. It can be almost anything: an idea, a suggestion to try out, a resource, some information—anything that shows that you are willing to invest something in the project *before* you get the business. Give them, or promise to give them, something of value during every call. "Even though we're not talking about JIT at this point, I put together an analysis of how MRP II compares with . . ." or, "When I get back to the office, I'll send you a copy of Senge's article . . ."

## CALL OBJECTIVE

A critical part of preparation is to clarify your call objective. This guideline holds true throughout the sales process. As a general rule, your call objectives should reflect what you want prospective customers to *give you*, not what you want to give them. The two things you will want most are specific information and opinions about ideas you have previously communicated. In this first call, you should have a very simple primary objective: to get the prospect to agree that there is value in meeting with you again (evidence of your prospect's *opinion* that what you have said has been valuable and that it makes sense to meet again). Anything more ambitious, such as trying to get delicate information, may be too much for the situation. You will achieve your primary objective when you accomplish three secondary objectives:

1. Gather enough information from the prospect to indicate that the prospect has a need for which you can provide a solution.
2. Begin to establish competence, credibility, and compatibility through the questions you ask, comments you make, and ideas you offer.
3. Demonstrate to your prospect that you understand the situation and conditions affecting his or her need.

## SEQUENCE OF EVENTS IN THE INITIAL CALL

Ideally, your prospect will talk more than you will in this initial call, because you should direct the flow of the call with your questions. Begin by asking your prospect about the Expressed Need, that is, your potential client's view of the situation. Do not offer your opinion about whether the need is valid. That can come later. Draw out a comprehensive description, and consider any opinions thoughtfully. Suppress your consultant's ego and admit to yourself that clients occasionally come up with good ideas. This may be one of those times. If you immediately discount the prospect's ideas, your ego has overcome your professional competence.

As mentioned earlier, your prospect may express the need in terms of a prescribed solution: "Our problem is that we don't have a strategic plan . . ." "We need better internal communication . . ." "Our project management system is obsolete . . ." "We need to scrap our executive compensation system and start all over." The prospect has expressed a need but it is not a true need, it is the desire to obtain a specific solution.

## Implementer Relationship

At this point, your prospect is probably talking to you because he or she wants someone to implement the prescribed idea, that is, a consultant who will say, "I understand what you have in mind, and I'll tell you how we can give you exactly what you want." You may not want to respond that way however, because of two conflicting interests: (1) You want the business; (2) you want to be perceived as an expert, not just an implementer. What's more, your professional ego won't let you automatically accept your potential client's solution as correct.

Nevertheless, resist the temptation to challenge the proposed solution. Consider your prospect's probable reaction if you immediately disagree and try to force yourself into an expert role. In a sense, it is a way of saying that you are more competent than your prospect. And, you can be sure that you have just given that prospect a good reason to widen the search for a consultant and to turn a possible noncompetitive or sole-source proposal into a competitive one. So, initially, go with the flow.

### Case History

I violated the preceding advice recently, and it turned out to be the correct strategy. But before I went against the flow, I discovered good reasons to do so. The company, a professional services firm, was interested in training their business developers—something that my firm is known for. From my experience, I have learned that companies frequently seek a training "fix" based on the logic that if a company is not being awarded as many contracts as it would like to win, the business developers must need more training. In such situations, I always search for symptoms other than low skill levels.

First, while waiting in the reception area, I looked through the company newsletter and saw that the firm's "Total Quality" activities were prominently reported. Next, I learned in the interview that this was a competitive opportunity, so I had to decide immediately when I should try to differentiate myself—now or later. Lastly, I discovered that my prospective client, although quite senior in the organization, was just completing his MBA and was currently studying organizational change. Because of what I had found out, I decided to try to change the flow from exploring training needs to exploring organizational issues that affect the firm's sales success. If I had not picked up that additional information, however, I would have continued to pursue my prospect's expressed needs.

## More Questions

Next, ask about the company, the business situation, your prospect's job, responsibilities, reporting structure, experience—the "environmental" information that allows you to put the expressed need into perspective. Through this broad conversation, you may discover other needs.

If you have time, go back to the Expressed Need again. Find out who else thinks it is important. Attempt to translate it into a Verified Need, that is, something of which there is too much or too little:

> You said you need a strategic plan; does that mean that too many of your managers are running off in conflicting directions?

> When you say you need to improve internal communication; does that mean that a lot of people don't have the information they need to do their jobs?

> You said that your project management system is obsolete; does that mean you are experiencing frequent quality problems, or budget overruns?

When you say you need to scrap your executive compensation system, does that mean you're paying your key people too much or too little? Are you losing the wrong people? Tell me what made you come to that conclusion.

If your interpretation has been correct, you will have begun to get the information that will *verify* the need. If your interpretation has been wrong, chances are your prospect will correct you. For example, when you questioned the need for better internal communication, the prospect might have answered: "No, our people think they get enough information to do their jobs, they just don't know where the company is going . . . if we're going to be sold, or merged, or what." You originally thought the communication problem might have something to do with work redesign. However, you have learned that it is something entirely different.

When you questioned the issue with the executive compensation situation, the answer could have been: "Frankly, I don't know what may be wrong with our executive compensation system. All I know is that our CEO came back from a conference in New York, said he had heard a speech from some guy named Paul Smith, and that we need to overhaul our system." So, you have learned of a felt need that is not verified by any facts. And, you have found a place to start.

If you don't get a confirmation or correction, or if your prospect insists on discussing only the possible solution, not the need, probe more deeply by suggesting some related experience. Ask your prospect to compare and contrast your experience with the expressed need. For example, "In a project that we were involved in last year, the client was concerned that . . . how similar is that to your situation?"

As you can see, you have started to solve the Perfect Sales Equation. You have tried to verify the Expressed Need by getting the prospect to describe it in terms of "too much" or "too little." You have tried to determine whether the need is felt by getting your prospect to tell you that the current state is unacceptable.

You probably won't have time to ask about how the buy will be made and who will make it and about competition; that's fine, because you want plenty left to discuss in your next visit.

But, be prepared to talk price and budget. A price discussion may seem premature, but your prospect may need some indication of your price, especially if this is possibly a sole-source engagement. In a competitive situation, you can probably delay price discussions until the next meeting unless your prospect pushes you. If you must talk price, offer a range, recognizing that your client will remember the low end and you will remember the high end. Or, see if you can turn the discussion from price to budget.

## Bringing Up the Budget

Even if your prospect does not ask you for a rough estimate, you should consider bringing up the subject of budget, especially if you are talking to someone who probably cannot fund the project without approval from higher up. You need to talk money at this early stage so that you can find out whether this project is real—that it has been funded, and for a reasonable amount. You can waste a lot of time chasing a project that exists only in someone's imagination.

Many professionals avoid budget discussions because they don't want to scare off the prospect, or possibly they are uncomfortable with their fees. These are poor reasons. A budget discussion gives you indicators of the value the prospect places on this engagement. Consider asking questions such as:

> Do you have a budget? Would you mind telling me what you are thinking of?

> I can understand why you don't want to tell us your budget and would want us to give you a price, but frankly, unless we know roughly what kind of value you put on a solution to this problem, we would be shooting in the dark. So, would you tell me what kind of money you've been talking about?

> If you haven't yet established a budget, can you tell me whose cost center will fund the project?

If your prospect will not talk money, you must wonder whether the project has much chance of being funded. Also, keep in mind that when a prospect gives you a budget figure, it's usually the low side of a range that has a stretch of 10 to 20 percent. Maybe even 25 percent.

## Provide Something of Value

Don't end your interview on a discussion of money. Give your prospect something. Describe the general approach you might take; mention the issues that you think are most important; or promise to dig up some information. Do anything that the client can interpret as value received from the call.

Before leaving, you must summarize what you've accomplished: what you've learned, what you need to think about, and what more you need to learn. This assures the prospect that progress was made and that another meeting is necessary.

## RATIONALE

Keep the first call short—about 30 to 45 minutes—and err on the side of taking less time than the client is willing to give you. You want to give the impression that you are busy, respectful of the prospect's time, that you have many more questions to ask, and that you are eager to meet again as soon as possible. Furthermore, you need time to interpret what you've learned, to figure out what more you need to know or clarify, and to start to build a sales strategy. Equally important, you can build your relationship more solidly through a series of short calls than with one long call.

If you stay for an hour or so, you will gather more facts than you can digest and may create the impression (with your prospect and with you) that you are ready to write a proposal. You are *not* ready, unless you're into writing generic proposals.

## Exception

On rare occasions, your prospect may convey such urgency that you feel you must return with a plan or a proposal as soon as possible. Before believing this sense of urgency, find out what has created it and whether the person you're talking to has the budget to pay for your services. If your prospect convinces you that you must act in a hurry, then do it and prove that you can respond with speed and quality.

## TEMPTATIONS

Since selling always takes longer than it should, you should be aware of some temptations that can damage your effectiveness.

### Taking Shortcuts

If you already know about the company and the industry, you may be tempted to shortcut the exploration part of your sales call. If you do, you will fail to demonstrate that you understand your prospect's needs. Every prospective client wants the opportunity to explain why "my situation is unique."

### Being Aggressive

If you feel confident that you have the solution to your prospect's need, you may be tempted to leap into a description of what you can provide. If you do, you will diminish your opportunity to build the relationship and demonstrate your competency. The most common and the most damaging consultant behavior that I have observed is the tendency to jump at any opportunity to offer a solution. When you offer a premature solution:

- You have a good chance of being wrong.
- You may not get the opportunity to come up with another solution.

### Selling through Credentials

You may try to establish your credibility by promoting your credentials or those of your firm in terms of experience and capabilities. In fact, many professionals begin an interview by saying, "Let me tell you a bit about . . ." While this information may be important, it is far more impressive when delivered *after* you have learned more about the project and can describe your credentials as they relate to a specific project. Too often, professionals spout irrelevant information in hopes of impressing a client. At this stage, no one cares how big you are, how many services you offer, how many offices you have. The prospect wants to know if you can demonstrate that you understand his or her needs. If you can't, nothing else matters.

Credentials are frequently dear to a professional's heart. Remember, however, that every credential you cite as a benefit has a downside to it as well:

> We're the largest firm of our type. (You think that proves you're successful; prospects may wonder whether their project will get lost or will be important enough to attract your best people.)

> We have a great deal of experience in your *industry*. (You think that proves you will come up with a workable solution; prospects may wonder if you will apply original thinking.)

> We're a small firm and you will be working with our principals. (You think that proves prospects will get the best people working on their project; prospects may wonder if you have any "bench strength" or if they will be paying principals' rates for work that staff consultants can do just as well.)

> We have nine offices in the United States, plus the United Kingdom, Germany, and Japan. (You think that proves you can draw on vast knowledge and experience from your farflung empire; prospects may think, "Who cares? We only have one plant and it's here in Springfield.")

The time to promote your credentials is after you have demonstrated that you understand your prospect's needs and can offer a solution with real benefits. Then, your prospect can rationalize everything about your firm or your offer:

> They're a huge firm, but they really understand our needs . . .

They're new to our industry, but they really understand our needs . . .

They're not local, but they really understand our needs . . .

They're expensive, but they really understand our needs . . .

## HURDLES

Sometimes your prospect interrupts your strategy and places hurdles in your way. For example:

Tell me about your firm. (Answer briefly, then continue with your questions.)

What's your background? (Answer briefly, then continue with your questions.)

I have a specific need: How would you approach this problem? (Answer, "We would need to know a lot more than we do right now to get specific, but this is the general approach we would probably take," and then outline the approach.)

Can you give me a quick proposal? (Answer, "No, we need to know more before we can do that." Any proposal that you write, even if "draft" is marked all over it, will probably be viewed by your prospect as a firm offering.)

## NEXT STEPS

As you will recall, your primary objective for this call was to get your prospect to agree that there's a good reason to meet with you again. Therefore, before concluding your meeting, get your prospect's commitment (date and time) to another appointment. No sales call should ever end without getting an agreement to a specific next step.

Before outlining an approach for conducting the "next step" interview, in the chapter that follows I will take you through ways to initiate business on your own.

# 8

# INITIAL CONTACT THROUGH SOLICITATION

This chapter focuses on your first contact with a prospect when you, the professional, have solicited it. You will see, first, how a social contact can lead to a solicitation and, second, how to conduct a cold call.

The theme implicit in all the tactics and techniques within this book—and especially in this chapter—is to avoid giving your prospect a reason to say *no* until you feel a high probability that he or she will say *yes*. You are most vulnerable to prospective clients' rejection at the initial contact because, at this point in your relationship, you and your prospects have the least amount of operational information. You know very little about your prospects and their needs. They know very little about you and your capabilities. Even more importantly, prospects may not know very much about their own needs. So, at this low level of mutual understanding, prospects can easily draw the conclusion that they don't have a need and/or that you don't offer the right capabilities.

## OBJECTIVE

Your objective for any initial contact is to get an appointment or to set up the means to get an appointment. If you attempt something more ambitious, you increase the probability of your prospect prematurely saying no.

## Social Functions

The initial contact can occur anywhere, and those who excel at business development keep their antennae active. Social situations often provide opportunities for initial business contacts.

### Case History—Saturday Night

While at a small dinner party, you meet a guest named Tom, who sounds as if he could be a potential client. At some point, you have an opportunity to ask Tom about his business. He appears to be a potential client or at least an important referral to potential clients, so you keep asking questions that lead to your area of interest. Your sense of social propriety guides you here; you carefully avoid probing questions that you would use in a business interview.

Eventually, your new acquaintance feels guilty about doing all the talking and asks what you do, which gives you an opportunity to position yourself as a possible resource. You briefly describe your business. If your new acquaintance had shown no interest, you would have kept asking questions about him or his business until he focused on your services or you became bored. Since he expresses interest in you as a possible resource, however, you divulge as little as possible because you know that the more you say, the greater the probability that he will make a premature conclusion about his needs or your capabilities. (Remember the Hierarchy of Sales Communication Media. Your initial contact may be a one-on-one conversation, but it is not in a good environment for mutual understanding.)

Your new friend eventually asks, "Do you ever do any of that kind of work with investment bankers?

"As a matter of fact, we do," you answer.

Tom then responds eagerly, "Let me tell you, we really need your kinds of services. I think half the time we're spinning our wheels, running off in three directions at once. So, how would you go about . . ."

"Frankly, Tom," you interrupt, ignoring his mixed metaphor, "you don't want to get me started talking because I can go on for hours. Instead, I'm not traveling at all next week, so why don't we get together for lunch, or better still, maybe we can spend an hour or so together in your office kicking around ideas. I can't tell you for sure that we have anything to offer you, but I'd really like to hear about what's going on. Do you have a card with you? Thanks, and here's mine. I'll give you a call Monday afternoon, and let's see if we can set something up."

A social situation is a terrible place to talk serious business. There are distractions, possibly the influence of alcohol, and you have had no time to do your homework. So, take the best you can get—an appointment or the reasonable expectation of an appointment.

In all initial contacts, provide just enough information so that you create the *probability* that a productive relationship could develop, but *not enough* information for the prospect to say no to a subsequent meeting.

### Case History—Monday Afternoon

On Monday afternoon, you follow up your Saturday night contact with a telephone call. Tom's secretary doesn't recognize your name and asks the nature of your call. You tell the secretary, "It's to follow up a conversation Tom and I had over the weekend."

When Tom gets on the phone, you make a quick reference to your past conversation, and try to schedule an appointment. He first says he would like you to meet some other people and plans to ask two or three others to join you, but you gently yet firmly decline. On the surface, this response may seem to violate a business-related eternal truth. With your knowledge of sales communication media, however, you know that you are not ready for a group meeting at this time.

"That's a nice suggestion, Tom. But, if you don't mind, I'd rather spend time with you. And, if it turns out that we have mutual interests, then I would really appreciate an introduction to the others."

A one-on-one, face-to-face conversation is the best way to begin a relationship because, this early in the relationship, you don't know enough to communicate effectively with a group, and the varied interests the group members may represent. At this point, you are most vulnerable to someone saying no although the actual words will be something like this: "Well, to be perfectly honest, that's just not a high priority with us right now."

## Business Functions

Essentially the same process that you use in social situations is appropriate for people you meet at business functions or other activities. You'll hear all kinds of stories about people who made big sales on airplanes, in cabs, at a chance meeting in a bar, and so forth, but that's not the way to bet (and they were probably selling widgets, not professional services). Don't try to create a legend—get an appointment.

## THE DREADED COLD CALL

Although professionals disagree on what's a cold call, what's a warm call, and what's a prospecting call, the majority seem to agree that they hate cold calling. But let's not worry about terminology. In the preceding chapter, we worked on situations when the prospects called you; here, we will work on the occasions when you call the prospect.

You have two reasons to call a prospect: (1) to introduce yourself as a potential valued resource, and (2) to offer an idea that you think may have value.

## Attitude

Consultants—even more than other salespeople—hate rejection because in rejecting your company or your services, the prospect seems to be rejecting *you*. When you cold call prospects, you have a good chance of getting rejected. The only way to soften this blow to the ego is to remind yourself that these prospects are not really rejecting you, they are saying no to an unfamiliar name and probably feel no need to give you their time. So, try to develop an attitude like that of the dedicated angler, as described in the wonderful little book, *The Spawning Run*.[1]

> Fishing demands faith. . . . To catch a fish you have to have faith that the water you are fishing in has got fish in it, and that you are going to catch one of them. You still may not catch anything; but you certainly won't if you don't fish your best, and you won't do this without faith to inspire you to do it. You won't approach the water carefully. You won't study the water carefully. You won't cast carefully. You won't fish out your cast; to do this, patience is required, and patience is grounded on faith. . . . Faith and faith alone can guard the fisherman against a demon of which he is particularly the prey, the demon of self-irony, from acquiescence in the opinion of the ignorant that he is making a fool of himself.

Unfortunately, your prospects don't make it easy for you to maintain the faith. You have to convince yourself that you must do your best on tasks that you may inherently dislike. And you have to convince yourself that you are not making a fool of yourself when you cold call.

It's easy to be critical of those people who won't return your calls, who don't remember the literature you sent them, and who only vaguely remember meeting you at some association meeting. But don't be critical. Be tolerant. Because if you are critical, by the time you finally get to talk to your prospect,

---

[1]Humphrey, William. 1970. *The Spawning Run*. New York: Knopf.

you'll be so angry that you'll jeopardize your chances of getting an appointment.

## Whom to Call

Try to get the name of the most senior person in the organization who would directly benefit from your services. This does not necessarily mean that you should try to get "to the top of the house," to the CEO, unless you know that the CEO would be involved in buying your services.

**Why Not Call the CEO?**   Many CEOs are familiar with good, contemporary management practices. They have read books on leadership, and they understand the necessity of empowering lower levels and pushing decision making down. Fortunately, you won't run into many CEOs today who run roughshod over their organizations, forcing favored outside resources on their subordinate. Or subordinates who try to curry favor by sending business to the boss's friends. If you get a referral to a CEO, use it, but not for selling a service that is a subordinate's responsibility. We will have more about this subject when we discuss the Buying Center in Chapter 9.

**Line or Staff?**   In many organizations, staff managers may buy a service, but line managers will use it. In that instance, the staff managers are easier to see. Their job descriptions probably state or imply that they are responsible for providing or acquiring the services you offer. However, ideally—and despite the risks of circumventing the staff person—you want to see the line person who uses your services.

Staff people, at best, have only secondhand knowledge of what line people do and need. As a result, they often cannot recognize the value of what you offer. Even worse, they may recognize your value and find it threatening. On the other hand, line people may not be interested in seeing consultants because they think that's a staff job.

**Prioritizing Line and Staff.**   Staff people are easier to see, but not as valuable to you; line people may be more difficult to see, but have greater value. So, first try to get an interview with the line manager most directly affected by your service. If you fail, then go to staff. When you must meet with staff people, chances are that you'll encounter some defensiveness. If you point out some problem, they may take it as criticism; so begin by describing your perception of an apparent need, and then ask for their opinion of its importance.

## Getting the Door Open

There are two schools of thought about calling for an appointment. One says you should send a short letter first and then make the telephone call; the other says forget the letter, just make the call. I use the letter for two reasons:

1. *Recognition.* I see an advantage in having some name recognition when I call. If I write a very short (one paragraph) letter, I have a moderately high probability that my prospect will read it and may remember my name when I call. This helps me over that first uncomfortable hurdle when I make my follow-up telephone call.
2. *Personal Motivation.* In my letter, I tell my prospect that I will call on a specific date, which forces me to make the telephone call. I, personally, need something that forces me to make the call because I always have a lot of good reasons why I am too busy to make cold calls.

**Introductory Letter.** I use the format in the following sample letter. Before writing, however, you must define your *entrée idea*, the appeal that will get you in the door. The entrée idea relates to the offering/solution position in the Perfect Sales Equation:

Dear _____:

Our firm specializes in _____, and we have recently developed some approaches that I think you will find interesting. I would like to meet with you briefly to discuss (entrée idea) and to explore whether our capabilities might be useful to you.

I will call you next _____ to ask for an appointment.

In my experience, this letter has a reasonably high probability of being read, understood, and of setting a favorable climate for my follow-up call. It is:

- Short (one paragraph).
- Simple (states exactly what I want).
- Relevant (relates to the reader's expected interests).
- Appealing (the entrée idea promises that some value may come from a brief meeting).

**Follow-Up Telephone Call.**   Everyone finds it difficult to get through to someone when your name is not known. Many secretaries are either directed to screen telephone calls, or they believe it is their moral duty and mission in life to screen calls. Regardless, they can be tough, as you probably well know.

Surefire techniques for getting through to a prospect do not exist—at least for me. I have read many books on selling and have attended many sales training seminars, and most of the surefire techniques I have been exposed to I would find embarrassing to use.

If you really want to get an appointment with someone, you have to be tenacious because (be honest) you may not be able to offer your prospect a compelling reason to see you. Chances are quite good, however, that you can eventually make your prospect (and/or the secretary) feel guilty because you have tried so hard and so long for an appointment. Or, one of them may just admire your tenacity. So call once a week, every week, until you get through to your prospect.

When you call and the secretary answers, "Mr. [Ms.] _____'s office" ask: "Is he [she] in please?" or "May I speak to her [him] please." Some sales literature says that you should refer to the person by his or her first name, but when the secretary asks "who's calling" and doesn't recognize your name, it will provide a good tip-off that it's a sales solicitation. If this causes the secretary to feel competitively protective, you will decrease your odds of getting through. On the other hand, you might fool the secretary. No best bet here.

If the secretary asks "Can Mr. [Ms.] _____ return your call," answer, "Yes, I would appreciate that, but with my schedule, I'll be hard to reach, and so I'll call back as well." Then, remember to ask, "Are you Mr. [Ms.] _____'s secretary? What is your name, please? When would be the best time to call back?" Now, you have begun to establish a personal relationship with the secretary, which can help a great deal.

On your next call, say: "Hi, [secretary's name], this is [your name], may I speak with Mr. [Ms.] _____?" As the secretary gets to know you over the phone, it becomes more likely that your messages will get through or that you can learn something useful about your prospect.

**"What Is This in Regard To?"**    This is a euphemism for "Who are you?" and is a tough screen to penetrate. I wish I knew a high-percentage technique to get through it. I have a few suggestions, however. First, prepare for that question . . . because, if you don't, you'll probably say something ineffectual such as, "I'm calling as a follow-up to a letter I wrote Mr. [Ms.] _____ last week." This may be true, but it won't get you through because the secretary is not really asking what you want. Rather, since your name is unfamiliar, the underlying question is whether you are important enough to let you through to the boss. So, say something like, "I am a management consultant with [your firm]. I am working on performance management systems, and I would like to speak with Mr. [Ms.] _____."

Mentioning a firm with a well-known name is often an effective approach. Theodore Levitt's valuable book *Industrial Purchasing Behavior*[2] published a study showing that the company name ("source effect" in communication) may be sufficient to get you a hearing.

---

[2]Levitt, Theodore. 1965. *Industrial Purchasing Behavior*, Boston, Harvard Business School.

If your firm name is not well known, emphasize your area of interest and maybe embellish it a bit: "I am a management consultant with [your firm]. I am working on performance management systems, and I believe that Mr. [Ms.] _____ has some interesting views on the subject. May I speak with him [her]?" This approach disguises your real intention but is not blatantly deceitful. And, in justification of bending your real purpose for calling, you know that a secretary who concludes you are trying to sell something will never let you through.

I've heard some aggressive business developers say that it doesn't matter what ruse you use to get to your prospect as long as you get there. I disagree. The most important quality a consultant can possess is integrity. If your initial contact lacks integrity, it will taint whatever relationship follows.

## At Last—Getting Through

Although rejection is part of cold calling, sometimes you're going to get through, so be ready. Write out ahead of time what you want to say; because you have only one opportunity, you will feel pressure, and you can easily stumble or say the wrong things. So, make a rough draft of what you want to say, but *don't read it*. If you do, you'll sound as if you're canvassing for home improvements. As shown in the following examples, what you say over the phone should paraphrase what you said in your letter (if you have used one):

### Specific Entreé Idea

Ms. _____, this is _____. I dropped you a note a few days ago mentioning that we have done some significant work lately helping privately held manufacturers with their strategic planning. I was hoping that we might spend 15 or 20 minutes telling you about some of the work we have done and seeing if you have an interest in our capabilities.

### General Appeal

Mr. _____, this is _____. I sent you a note last week saying that our firm specializes in human resources consulting, and we have identified (name of prospect's company) as a firm we would very much like to do business with. I would like to stop by to introduce myself, give you an idea of the types of services we offer, and to see if we could become a valued resource to you in the future.

**Special Situation**

Ms. _____, this is _____. I dropped you a note last week saying that we have just opened a new office (or started a new service, or recently developed a new system, etc.). I'd like you to think of us as a potential resource, and I'd like to stop by and introduce myself and my firm's capabilities.

**When You Can't Think of Anything Else and Can't Get a Referral**

Mr. _____, this is _____ from _____. We have identified a few companies that we would eventually like to do business with, and I'd like to stop by and introduce myself. I'm not going to try to sell you anything, but I would like to meet you. Could you give me 10 minutes of your time next week?

## Suggestions for Dealing with Potential Problems

**Requests for Literature.** If your prospect stalls in scheduling an appointment and asks if you could send some literature, answer politely, "No." Again, write out your response ahead of time so that you word it exactly the way you want it. Think through why you do *not* want to send or even deliver literature by asking yourself some hard questions:

• Is a brochure a rich or lean medium?
• What's the likelihood that your prospect will spend time reading your literature?
• If your prospect spends time reading your literature, will your brochure say anything that your competitor's brochure doesn't say?

- Is your brochure any more credible than all the other brochures the prospect receives?
- If your prospect doesn't read the brochure, or doesn't believe what it claims, what response will you get when you call again?

At best, asking you to send literature may indicate a mild anxiety about spending time with you or, at worst, provide a polite way of rejecting you. So, use this opportunity to do the unexpected—say no. An explanation such as the following tells the prospect that no brochure can represent your services:

> I don't want to send you a brochure because our services are customized, and frankly, I don't think a brochure can adequately describe them. But, I think if we could spend just a few minutes together, we'll both know whether I have anything of value to offer. (Pause) So, can we set up an appointment for early next week? I have some time on . . .

Avoid the cliche, "Would next Monday afternoon or next Tuesday be best?" That approach identifies you as a peddler. Also, don't offer to drop literature by with the hope of turning it into a visit. You can bet your prospect will be "tied up" when you arrive, and you will have just functioned as a very expensive postage stamp.

**Requests for Additional Information.** If your prospect says, "Yes, I might be interested in getting together, but can you tell me a little about your company?" just give a bare-bones description and then follow with some comment like "and in our marketing plan, we identified your company as a firm we would really like to do business with." That switches the subject right back to your appointment.

In a more difficult scenario, your prospect says, "Yes, I might be interested in getting together, but first tell me a little about what you have in mind?"

This is a highly vulnerable point. If you say the wrong thing, your prospect can conclude either that he or she has no need or you have nothing to offer; and if you don't say something, your prospect has no reason to schedule the appointment. So, go back to your original reason for requesting the appointment: "In general, I'd like to talk about what we have been doing in strategic planning for privately held manufacturing firms, but mostly, I am interested in getting to know you and in having you know something about us."

You haven't answered your prospect's question *literally,* but you have answered it *conceptually* by indicating that you aren't going to come in and try to sell some ready-made solutions for special situations. What's more, you have told the truth. Or, at least it will be the truth if you follow the sequence described in the following chapter.

# 9

# WORKING THE PERFECT SALES EQUATION

The good news is that you obtained the appointment. The bad news is that it could be a very short relationship unless you do something smart with it.

Because your would-be client did not initiate the contact, you must recognize that he or she does not feel a need for your services, regardless of your credentials, capabilities, and experience. You have yet to prove that your services have any value until your prospect can see the connection between your services and the solution of a felt need. So, forget all that you may have read in Salesmanship 101 about beginning your conversation with a benefit statement—a benefit is not a benefit unless it resolves a verified and felt need, and right now you don't know if your prospect has a need. This person did agree to see you, however, so lurking somewhere may be a need; this is your opportunity to uncover it.

Your obvious short-term objective is to find out if your prospect has a need for the service you described in your entrée

idea. In addition, you want to establish yourself as a valued resource, someone with relevant capabilities. So, even if this call
does not pay off with the possibility of an immediate assignment, it should lead to future business or referrals. This chapter
will address both objectives: developing your entrée idea into a
need, and establishing yourself as a valued resource.

## CALL PREPARATION

Do it. Chapter 7 described why preparation is important before
meeting with a prospect who has called you. Where you have
solicited the contact, preparation is even more important. You
need to establish yourself as a thoughtful professional, and the
more junior you are, the more preparation you need. Read your
prospect's annual report, check the *Readers' Guide to Periodical
Literature* at your local library for current new articles. Pull a
Dun and Bradstreet report and check appropriate industry direc-
tories. Besides acquiring useful information, you will develop
self-confidence from doing your homework. Regardless of your
seniority, you will create a favorable impression by citing recent
facts relevant to your prospect's firm or industry.

## WORKING YOUR OBJECTIVES

Your primary objective is to get the prospect's opinion of your
entrée idea and its applicability to conditions within his or her
organization. You cannot concentrate solely on that objective,
however, because you also want to establish yourself as a valued
resource, and you want to find out what other, higher priority
needs may exist. If you focus only on your entrée idea, you won't
have anywhere to go if a verified or felt need does not develop.

### Starting the Interview

Unless you pick up some clue that your prospect wants to engage
in small talk for awhile, begin to describe your entrée idea as

briefly as is practical. The more detailed your description, the more likely that your idea will be off base. You are not selling anything at this point, you are using your entrée idea as a pump primer to get your prospect to talk. Therefore, after your brief description, use a transitional question such as, "Rather than going into details, let me ask you how the [entrée idea] relates to the conditions here at [prospect's firm]?"

If your entrée idea has struck a need, your prospect may move into an enthusiastic description of what's wrong, including an interpretation of the unacceptable current situation. If so, go with it, remembering that while you may be establishing a need, you have not yet established yourself as a valued resource. On the other hand, the response of a cautious prospect may be positive, but not as revealing. Take that opportunity to shift the conversation and learn more about what's going on in the prospect firm. Ask insightful questions that indicate your professional competence and reflect a sincere interest in the prospect and the company, not just a means for finding an opening for a sales pitch. Be willing to explore because you may discover an *apparent need* that is more urgent and important than the one you associated with your entrée idea.

## Investigating Change

Most organizations are undergoing some sort of change driven by the highest level of the organization. The nature of that change may reveal an *overriding corporate goal.* The goal will support high-priority projects to which you may be able to connect your entrée idea or perhaps another idea or need. Whether or not you discover such an overriding corporate goal, showing broad interests will help establish you as a valued resource.

## Changing Your Prospect's Perception

Frequently consultants get typecast into a limited specialty, and the prospect can't perceive them in a different role. This can be a problem when your entrée idea does not seem to fit in with the reputation of your firm. A good example would be a benefit plans consultant who wants to be thought of as having broader human resources consulting capabilities. The consultant could simply say, "You may know our firm only as benefit consultants, but lately we've been doing a great deal of work in other human resources assignments such as succession planning and job re-design." That statement would have a great deal more credibil-ity, however, if it followed a line of insightful questions related to human resources and outside the client's perceived range of competence for the consultant.

## Congruence: What You Sell and How You Sell It

An extremely effective partner of a national public accounting firm told me that the time spent with the prospect before you submit your proposal or engagement letter provides a free sample of your service. That statement has many implications worth exploring.

How you sell says more about you and your firm than the claims you make in a proposal or a brochure:

- If you want your client to believe your claim that "we listen," then you had better demonstrate excellent listening behavior while selling.
- If your firm takes pride in delivering "quality service dedi-cated to specific client needs," then you would be ill-advised to come up with a quick, generic solution.
- If you want your potential client to believe you are "responsive to your special circumstances," figure out some way you can, in fact, respond to those circumstances.

Each interview situation presents different opportunities, but an almost universal way of showing responsiveness and "value added" service is to spend time discussing your prospect's needs and circumstances, and giving extra service. In other words, you demonstrate what it is like to work with you.

## GIVING IT AWAY

Now, by spending hours of front-end time discussing a prospect's needs, you can be guilty of giving away what you think you should be paid for. You and I, and every other consultant I know, would agree: You should be paid for the time spent in helping a prospect identify and clarify needs. Unfortunately, most clients don't agree. They object to paying a consultant for a discussion of something that they are not sure exists. Or, they say, "Why should I pay you to learn my business?" which doesn't make any sense but indicates a reluctance to pay for activities not directly related to a deliverable.

Some consultants estimate that they "give away" 10 to 15 percent of the engagement before they even get the work. You may be able to recover some or all of this time once you get the engagement, so keep track of your preengagement time. But unless the prospect has called you, giving away some front-end services "goes with the territory." When the prospect initiates the contact indicating an expressed need, you can sometimes charge for a formal "needs analysis" or a feasibility study. When you initiate the contact—and you want the business—you may have to do some digging for free.

## BUILDING CREDIBILITY

Furthermore, remember that you sell intangible services. In doing so, you ask your prospect to *buy a description* of what you will deliver and to *accept your promise* that your services will meet your prospect's needs, budget, and time schedule. That is a risky buying decision. To build the credibility and trust necessary for your prospect to make such a decision, you have to do something more than talk about all the clients who have used your services profitably in the past. Your prospective client, who is smart enough to know you won't mention any clients who have not profited from your past services, must determine your trustworthiness from your present behavior. Unless you're a rainmaker, you will need a few calls to develop solid credibility (and not everyone trusts rainmakers on the first call).

## TECHNIQUES

When a prospect calls you, it stands to reason that the prospect should do most of the talking. But when you have gained the interview on the strength of your entrée idea, you will feel a great temptation to take control and really sell that idea. Avoid the temptation. You still must get the prospect to talk so you can learn enough to make your idea relevant.

In an approach that is even worse than describing their idea at length, some professionals open the interview by "positioning" their firm or stating their own credentials. Their purpose in providing this descriptive monologue is to (roll of drums) Establish Credibility.

Establishing credibility by association or claims is an outmoded convention still practiced by many professionals; it is driven by tradition, ego, or insecurity. Years ago, describing your firm and your credentials to get attention may have served a purpose. In today's business world, credentials are commonplace. What credentials can you offer that will cause your prospect automatically to believe you? That you have a PhD? That your firm has 300 professionals from seven disciplines and has served clients in the financial services community for the past 24 years? At this point in the relationship, who really cares besides you? Do you really think that a prospect decides to listen to you or believe you because you can recite past history? That tactic doesn't work for at least four reasons:

1. Credentials have no meaning unless they are attached to a scope of work. At this point in your relationship, the prospect doesn't know much about your idea, let alone the scope of work that would deliver the idea.

2. Your prospect may be prejudiced against your credentials or the credentials of your firm. For example, does your prospect like to work with large firms or small firms? Does this person

admire PhDs or think they are too academic? Is the would-be client impressed by people with 25 years' experience, or do some fresh perspectives offer more appeal? You don't know. So, why provide an opportunity to exercise prejudices? Unless absolutely forced to describe your own or your firm's credentials, don't say a word about them yet.

3. In reciting credentials, you are unlikely to find anything to say that's startling or even terribly interesting. Why begin your sales call with something rather dull?

4. You lose the opportunity to describe your capabilities and credentials *after* your prospect has shown an interest in what you can do. As mentioned before, this is the time when you get the greatest impact from your credentials because you can describe them in ways that support the ideas just discussed with the prospect.

Waiting to state your credentials after you and your potential client have agreed on the needs and after you have offered an attractive solution gives those credentials real power. They build confidence in the validity of your solution, and provide reasons for believing that you can do what you say you can do. What's more, after you have demonstrated that you may be able to provide something of value, the prospect's prejudices will disappear or will be rationalized because of the desire to work with you.

## PRIMARY CRITERION

Today's sophisticated buyers have a primary criterion: to buy from a professional who can demonstrate understanding of their needs. ("Demonstrate," an active verb, is not synonymous with "claim".) You can claim to be the biggest, the oldest, the fastest growing, the cheapest, the most convenient, the nicest, the smartest . . . whatever. All these attributes are mostly meaningless unless you demonstrate that you understand your prospect's needs. The single exception is the request for proposal (RFP) situation where the client doesn't give you much of a chance to demonstrate that you understand anything, and, as a result, buys the lucky best idea, the most impressive credentials, the most politically connected service, or the lowest price.

## USING THE PERFECT SALES EQUATION

You began your call with a brief description of your entrée idea. If the prospect did not enthusiastically describe a need situation, you moved quickly into asking insightful questions for the following three reasons:

1. You wanted to create the impression of competence and professionalism.
2. You wanted to find out if your prospect has needs that you hadn't anticipated.
3. You wanted your prospect to perceive you in ways other than those conveyed by your firm's reputation.

If your prospect showed a real interest in your entrée idea, that gave you the license to zero in on needs . . . to find out what sparked the interest. To find out, you need to ask questions, many of which can be prepared ahead of time.

To prepare your questions, refer to the Perfect Sales Equation. What facts, in general, could you verify to help relate your idea to your prospect's situation? For example, if your idea is a cash management study, what facts would indicate whether the firm's current cash management system is functioning effectively or ineffectively? If you offer cash management services and you're talking with the treasurer of a firm that you know does not have a lockbox system, you might say: "Let's go back to the primary reason for my call. We have found that by setting up a lockbox system in firms of your size and geographic dispersion, we can take anywhere from a day to three days out of their collection float, with obvious benefits to their cash flow. But, at this point, I haven't any reason to believe that you have a need to improve your cash flow."

Then, be prepared to listen to your prospect rationalize the current system—how it was developed; why it worked well in the past; why they have maintained it. When given a chance, every prospect will tell you, "We're just a little bit different—I think you'll find us somewhat unique." Never will you hear a prospect tell you, "We're just like everyone else in our industry—no difference. Anything that works for them will work for us."

Because of your experience, you can recognize the symptoms of problems quickly and you have seen many similarities among companies, but don't let your experience stop you from asking the questions that demonstrate to your prospect that you understand the firm's "unique" situation. Remember, *insightful questions build your credibility.* Equally important, prospects do not want to hear that their current approach is wrong or outdated until you have earned the right to an opinion by listening to a thorough description of the firm's present circumstances.

After having listened carefully you can test out the verifiable benefit on the Perfect Sales Equation model. You can say, "We find that it's not uncommon for companies such as yours to begin using a bank lockbox for payment processing, and if this is the case, then we can predict saving at least one day's worth of float. In your case, this could mean increased earnings up to $25,000 per year."

Then, explore the felt benefit: "It seems to me that such a savings would be worth dismantling [adapting or changing] your current system, but I may have missed something." Your goal, here, is to get your prospect to agree with you, which indicates a felt benefit. If you can accomplish this much in your first call, you have made significant progress.

## CALLS WITHOUT AN ENTRÉE IDEA

If you have an active referral network, you will have opportunities to call on prospects without resorting to an entrée idea.

While it may appear to be an advantage, without the focus of an entrée idea, many good discussions fail to bring a need to the surface, that is, the prospect does not describe an undesirable current situation. So, you may have to resort to either of the following plans:

- In Plan A, give your prospect something to respond to. For example, you might say something like: "We've been talking for some time now, and I'm surprised that you haven't mentioned any concerns about . . ." Or, "Our clients often ask us to develop "X," and I'm interested in your opinion . . ." Or, maybe you can use Plan B.
- In Plan B, you tell some relevant, interesting "war stories" to stimulate discussion. For example, a consultant I know worked at Texas Air during the acquisition of Eastern and Continental Airlines, and through the strike and spin-off attempts of Eastern. She has a wealth of referral connections as well as stories that she uses to set the stage, and then she says, "Of course, Texas Air was an extreme situation, but my guess is that many companies—and possibly yours—are experiencing much of the same . . ."

While war stories make for great conversation starters, respect the caveat not to disclose confidential information.

## ENDING YOUR CALL

As in the prospect-initiated call strategy, I encourage you to end your call after 30 to 45 minutes. If you weigh pros and cons of this time limit, logic will favor the pros.

Your long-term goals are to establish credibility and develop a relationship. You need multiple calls for both. If you have "shot your wad" on the first call, you will have difficulty creating a reason for the next call.

Your prospect may not voice every concern, even remember all of them, the first time you meet. If you have been fortunate enough to uncover a need, chances are your potential client thinks it is complex and not easily resolved. Therefore, if your first call goes from exploring needs to offering a solution, the client may believe your solution is poorly conceived.

On the other hand, it may seem against the laws of nature to end a call voluntarily when you're on a roll and your prospect is making encouraging noises. But do it anyway. If the deal is as solid as it appears, it won't disappear, and your probability of getting a buying decision to stick becomes much greater.

## SAVE YOUR SOLE SOURCE

Seller-initiated calls often result in sole-source assignments. We all have the fear, however, that at some point our prospect will invite competitors to propose on our carefully developed idea. Or, even worse, the prospect will take our idea and turn it into an in-house project. Neither occurrence is avoidable nor are they necessarily disasters.

In the case of competitive proposals, if you have done a careful job of selling and have built relationships as well as offered a valued service, you should have a strong advantage. Your competitors will probably be forced to submit a proposal without the benefit of researching the situation or building a relationship.

If your prospect takes your idea to in-house resources, be gracious. Maybe your prospect knows that what you proposed is well within the capabilities of internal resources and so spending money outside is not justifiable. Stay in touch; offer help to the in-house people; and try to build a sense of obligation. It's a good bet that you'll eventually get some business.

## LONG-TERM VALUE

Many seller-initiated calls produce no business at all. At the least, however, you have started to build a relationship that may pay off in the future. I have one relationship that has produced a great many profitable referrals over the years although I haven't done any business at all with the person who continues to give me those referrals. I know quite a few professionals who try to avoid prospecting. But I don't know any successful professionals who do.

# 10

# THE BUYING CENTER AND TYPE OF BUY

It seems obvious that you should try to identify the players involved in the buying decision before you submit a proposal, but failing to do so is common even among experienced business developers. Sometimes you can't find out who the players are, and sometimes you think you know but learn later that there are more and far higher level players than you could have imagined.

By definition, the Buying Center includes those people who interact for the purpose of making a buying decision[1]. Each person may fill more than one buying function and more than one person may fill each function.

It's a safe bet that both you and your initial contact (the initiator) will unwittingly create the illusion that you two are the only two in the game. You want to believe that because it makes your sales job much easier and less time consuming. The initiator

---

[1]Webster, Frederick E., Jr., and Wind, Yoram. 1972. *Organizational Buying Behavior* (p. 77). Englewood Cliffs, NJ: Prentice-Hall.

wants to believe that because it appeals to his ego. Although it is normal to entertain the illusion for a short time, you cannot focus sales efforts on only one person.

## THE PLAYERS

We can divide Buying Center members into two roles: the decision maker(s) and the influencers. You can expect one or two decision makers, at most, even if you're selling to a committee. If you are selling to a task force, there may be no decision makers, but that's another story (see Appendix A).

### Decision Makers

How can you tell a decision maker from the influencers? One good indicator is that your fee comes out of the decision maker's budget. Another indicator is that the decision maker is the person who gets the most badly burned if you fail. Only the decision maker can say "yes," whereas an influencer's power is limited to "no," or "I will recommend it."

### Influencers

You'll encounter several types of influencers:

1. The most important is the *User.* Users are those influencers who benefit most from the work you will do. For example, if you are selling a sales reporting system, the sales manager is probably the user, and the decision maker is probably the director of MIS (Management Information Systems).
2. *Technical influencers* are those who have some knowledge of your project and are in the position of evaluating your process, experience, credentials, and so forth.
3. *Political influencers* just try to swing the decision to some favored supplier—the apocryphal brother-in-law or someone they have worked with in the past. Political influencers can be hard to spot.

4. *Initiator* is another type of influencer and often has been delegated by the decision maker to seek a supplier. The initiator is likely to be a *gatekeeper,* who can open or close doors for you. The initiator may also take on the role of *coach* or *advocate.* This role can be paradoxical. While you can appreciate having someone trying to help, sometimes the coach's or advocate's help goes awry. More about that later.

5. *Ratifiers* are tricky. Usually the decision maker reports to the ratifier. For example, the chief executive officer (CEO) reports to the board of directors; the chief financial officer (CFO) reports to the CEO. You seldom have to worry about ratifiers except when you are replacing a long-standing supplier, or when you are not an obvious choice. For example, a ratifier might ask the decision maker, "Why are we hiring an accounting firm to do market research?"

6. In smaller and privately held companies, make sure you ask about *nonemployee influencers,* such as attorneys, bankers, outside investors, family members.

## IDENTIFYING THE BUYING CENTER

I have heard of many questions to ask when trying to identify the buying center. The following are ones I don't particularly like:

> Who besides you will be instrumental in the decision? (opinion)
>
> Who else should I be talking to about this project? (opinion)
>
> How many copies of the proposal should I prepare, and where should I send them? (indirect)

I like asking a couple of people this question: "Tell me how you [your organization] will go about making the decision." Then I really pin people down on the specifics, especially when I hear something like this: "I'll discuss this with a few people and get their input; then we'll have to run it by Charlie, and it's a done deal."

This is the time to unpack the abstract verbs and nouns, as described in Chapter 6, using questions like these:

Whom *specifically* will you discuss it with?

What's their interest in the project?

How will they react? What's going to turn them on, and what's going to turn them off?

Can any of them kill the project?

Assuming everything looks good, how do you plan to run it by Charlie?

Does Charlie make the final decision?

How is Charlie likely to react?

How about the others you discuss this with, will they talk to Charlie, too?

When you ask about the buying process, you not only get the names of the players, but the sequence in which their influence will be felt. This helps you set priorities regarding who in the Buying Center you will contact.

## INFLUENCING THE BUYING CENTER

If you were a full-time seller, you might have enough time to reach all the influencers. Since you're not, however, you have to decide whom you must see. As a general rule, if you're calling on only one person, that's not enough. First of all, you can't take just one person's opinion about the constituents of the Buying Center. Second, the first person you see may be the weakest player in the Buying Center. At minimum, you should call on the decision maker and the user. If they are the same person, look for that person's key advisor (either inside or outside the organization).

For the moment, we'll assume that you have the freedom to call anyone you like within the Buying Center for an interview.

I have found an effective approach begins by identifying yourself and the project, and then saying, "I understand that you have an interest in the project, and I'd like to spend some time with you to get your point of view." Except when trying to reach senior management or the decision maker, this approach will almost always work.

There have always been barriers to reaching influencers or decision makers high in an organization; the first one may be in your own head. It's beyond the scope of this book to speculate why some people have difficulty establishing high-level contacts or to suggest ways to overcome that problem. If you have the problem, I advise you to work to resolve it, because it will always limit your business development success.

Another barrier to high-level contact is inaccessibility. Many senior executives think it's not their role to talk to vendors or consultants. Furthermore, the management theories that promote "pushing decision making down" and "empowerment" help justify inaccessibility. On the other hand, if senior management has truly pushed decision making down or empowered subordinates, the Buying Center should be identifiable and its members easy to see.

In the past, a good general rule was to sell at the highest level possible—the CEO. Before using all your wiles to get a CEO interview, however, try to determine just how important it is. If you do get a CEO interview, be sure to talk CEO talk, not project talk; discuss the strategic and long-term implications of the project, not the project itself. If you question your ability to get a CEO interview because you lack seniority, involve a senior member of your firm.

## Be Prepared to Slow Down the Process

I know this recommendation sounds like a crime against nature. It's not, because unless you control the development of the buying process, nobody will buy anything. By "slow down the process," I mean hold off submitting a proposal until you thoroughly comprehend the sales situation. Usually, more people will influence the purchasing decision than you initially know about; there will be more competition (from other internal or external sources or from other demands on the budget) than you initially are prepared for.

Because you are selling an intangible, presumably a solution to a problem, each member of the Buying Center will perceive the problem differently and, therefore, perceive the value of your solution differently. The range of perception may run from full advocacy to complete rejection. So, don't let your sense of urgency and enthusiasm cause you to suggest a solution or write a proposal until you have had face-to-face conversations with key members of the Buying Center. Slow down the process!

## Beware of Coaches and Advocates

Any influencer may take on the additional role of coach or advocate, which, on the surface, seems to be a fortunate occurrence. However, while a coach may guide you through the organizational maze, an energetic advocate can also set you up for failure.

An advocate may offer to help you sell, saying something like, "I'll be over at R&D on Thursday; let me run the idea by Dr. Taylor." Wonderful, you think. It will save you some time, and having an inside advocate gives your idea credibility. Maybe. But, more likely, you have just turned your sale over to an incompetent. You'll never know how well the person represents your idea, and if something goes sour, you'll never know why. What is certain, however, is that your advocate will drop his or her advocacy the moment it becomes apparent that it is politically wise to do so.

Even if you don't have an advocate who tries to take control of the sale, your coach may encourage you to take the path of least resistance, by interviewing only certain people or writing a "preliminary" proposal.

Eager coaches may try to persuade you to write a proposal before you have had face-to-face sales conversations with key members of the Buying Center. Be prepared to take a firm stand. Tell your coach that you think it is premature to write a proposal—you need to gather more information.

This may be the most stressful point in the sales process. Your coach probably does not understand the sales process as well as you do and may advise you to proceed in a way that you know will court failure. So, you must make a difficult decision. Do you hazard alienating your prime supporter, or do you risk losing control of the sale?

Each situation poses special problems, and therefore, I can't advise you conclusively in one direction or the other. However, I can help you understand how many people rationalize the decision not to risk alienating their advocate or coach. One of the more enduring maxims of selling says "never alienate your prospect," with corollaries such as:

- Don't go around or over the head of your client contact.
- Beware of company politics.
- It's unprofessional to be pushy.
- Build the relationship and the transactions will take care of themselves.

Since you have plenty else to do—including keeping your billable time up—you are already conditioned to rationalize following the path of least resistance. In your conditioned state, you're ready to agree when your contact tells you that others won't see you and that he or she can test out the idea with some key people. What's more, the statements have the ring of truth. But almost always, you should resist the temptation.

## Getting to High-Level Influencers

Some consultants seemingly have no difficulty getting appointments with the most senior people in the client organizations; others seem to have a great deal of difficulty. While no particular communication style is better than any other when it comes to selling, people who can be very assertive have a huge advantage when trying to reach decision makers. They don't allow obstacles, which are more "head games" than real, to deter them from reaching the people they need to see.

Before going further, let's take a real case, do some analysis and try to come up with a strategy. As with almost every sales situation you will encounter, you cannot attribute the difficulty to one specific problem, such as the Buying Center. In this case, the management consultant believed the problem related to the Buying Center, but you will recognize other issues as well.

## Case History

The client is a manufacturer of consumer electronics with sales in excess of $100 million. The firm became a client about eight years ago when the management consultant assisted in a leveraged buyout. The consultant has done a few projects for the firm since then and is well known to the firm's small group of executive management. Key players are the VP-Manufacturing and VP-Finance, who both report directly to the CEO. The Corporate Controller and Manager-Electronic Data Processing report to VP-Finance.

The consultant's strongest relationship has been with VP-Finance (VP-FIN) and the Corporate Controller. The consultant has worked with VP-Manufacturing (VP-MFG), but only on projects initiated by the VP-FIN. Because of this, the consultant thinks the VP-MFG sees the consulting firm as the VP-FIN's "people."

Both the VP-FIN and VP-MFG have told the consultant in the past that the company needs a Manufacturing Resource Planning (MRP) system, and from past experience with the firm and knowledge of MRP, the consultant agrees.

The VP-MFG appears to be the decision maker because he can get approval from the CEO to fund the purchase of an MRP system. However, the consultant feels that it would jeopardize the relationship with VP-FIN if the project were not worked through from the Finance side of the house. Because of their past strong relationship, the consultant believes VP-Finance can help sell the VP-MFG on the MRP system.

To complicate matters, the Manager-EDP and the Corporate Controller have asked for funds to implement bar coding that they think will resolve the inventory control and production scheduling problem. The consultant disagrees. The Manager-EDP is an outspoken opponent to MRP.

The consultant has stated the problems as:

- Working with the personalities; getting to the decision maker (VP-MFG) without hurting the current relationship with VP-FIN.
- Developing the necessary relationship with the VP-MFG.
- Getting the opportunity to explore the firm's needs more fully.

What do you think? Has the consultant identified the decision maker? Should the consultant try to use VP-FIN as an advocate? Has the consultant really identified the problem? Although this case provides very little information and a lot of room for speculation, certain factors seem evident.

First, it is unlikely that the VP-MFG is the decision maker, since he must get approval to fund the project from the CEO. Furthermore, the Manager-EDP and the Corporate Controller have requested funding for a bar coding project. Who will give that approval? If it is the CEO, then we can build a strong case that the CEO will also be the decision maker for an MRP proposal.

Second, it is too soon for the consultant to push the sale of an MRP system. If management has been talking about an MRP system for some time but has not initiated action, the Verified and Felt Needs are not yet strong enough. An MRP system is one solution; the Manager-EDP and Controller think bar coding is another solution. Without better verification of the real need, neither solution is likely to be bought.

The consultant is probably mistaken in trying to develop the VP-FIN as an advocate because MRP is a manufacturing responsibility. If the VP-MFG feels the need strongly enough and can verify it, the VP-FIN does not have to be a major influence. The consultant has done a pretty good job of recognizing the potential conflict between the buying influencers. The Manager-EDP is a good example of a technical influence, with strong views on the MRP system itself, but not on the function it performs. Nevertheless, what looks like a Buying Center problem will probably smooth out once the consultant begins working with the VP-MFG to verify the need.

## TYPE OF BUY

Almost every buying situation can be categorized as one of three types of buy: Straight Re-Buy, Modified Re-Buy, and New Buy.[2] They differ from each other the following ways:

- The amount of risk associated with the buy.
- The probable size and composition of the Buying Center.
- The number and types of alternatives the Buying Center will consider in making the buying decision.

Because of these differing characteristics, different sales strategies must be used for each type. After you fully understand the three types of buy, you'll see how you can shape your strategy for each one.

The designation of type comes from the buyer's relationship with the project. For example, a newly hired Vice President-Human Resources may engage consultants to do an organizational climate survey. The VP's new firm has never done one before, but the VP conducted climate surveys twice before with a previous employer. If the VP-HR makes the buying decision, it is a Re-Buy, either Straight or Modified. If the CEO makes the decision, however, it's a New Buy.

In another example, a hospital's new VP-Development has never been involved in building new facilities, but the CEO has delegated to this person the task of writing the request for proposal and making the short-list decision. This is a New Buy situation, even though the hospital has expanded its facilities in the past.

### Straight Re-Buy

A Straight Re-Buy can be either a repeat or replacement. You don't need to analyze the repeat buy, because it occurs when the buyer buys the same service from the same source. A

[2]Robinson, Patrick J., Faris, Charles W., and Wind, Yoram. 1967. *Industrial Buying Behavior and Creative Marketing.* Boston: Allyn & Bacon.

## TYPES OF BUYS

### Straight Re-Buy

Buying Center: Small and usually low-level; initiator may also be decision maker.

Need to be Understood: High; confirm expectations.

Need for Information: Low.

Decision Risk: Low; verified needs should document problems with incumbent vendor relationship and performance history.

Potential Alternatives: Quality, service, price.

Solution Stability: Good; look for political influencers.

### Modified Re-Buy

Buying Center: Wide and mid-level; must work with user.

Need to be Understood: High; confirm new specifications and expectations.

Need for Information: Moderate; confirm reason to modify the re-buy.

Decision Risk: Moderate; prospect has experience with service.

Potential Alternatives: Few, easily identified.

Solution Stability: Good; stress ability of service to match new needs.

### New Buy

Buying Center: Complex and high level; must work with the decision maker.

Need to be Understood: High; continue to monitor prospect's assumptions and expectations.

Need for Information: High; must educate.

Decision Risk: High, subject to change; must maintain close contact throughout decision-making process.

Potential Alternatives: Many, varied.

Solution Stability: High uncertainty, requires documentation of verifiable benefits.

replacement buy, however, occurs when the buyer considers buying the same service from a different source.

The purchase of an annual audit is probably a Straight Re-Buy. In this situation, the Buying Center is probably small, and the initiator may in fact be the decision maker. This is a low-risk buy, because the buyer knows exactly what he or she wants and knows how to evaluate potential sources. The decision, once made, is unlikely to be changed. Nor do you need to educate the buyer. But, you do need to find out why he or she will consider changing sources because that will tell you the decision maker's needs.

In Straight Re-Buys, the professional service is a requirement, not a need. Whether you are the incumbent provider or the competitor, look for some dissatisfaction within the current situation that relates to price, quality, or service. These are the second order needs you read about in Chapter 3. If you can find or develop a Verified and Felt Need, you will have a good probability of retaining or acquiring the business.

## Modified Re-Buy

In this situation, someone in the Buying Center—probably the user—has said that conditions have changed so that a Straight Re-Buy will not satisfy specific needs. It's a higher risk buy because the purchase will include some new elements. The Buying Center will include more influencers, and the user will be most important.

Hiring a consulting firm to design a performance-based compensation system probably qualifies as a Modified Re-Buy, presuming that the decision maker has previously used consultants to design compensation systems. If you are looking at sales performance, the primary user is probably the executive responsible for business development or relationship management; the VP-Human Resources is probably the decision maker.

In this situation, some client education will be needed, especially with the user. Also, you must clarify the user's expectations. Expect the decision maker to explore alternative solutions, such as make-or-buy or sample test.

## New Buy

These opportunities make professionals salivate. Your client has little choice but to treat you as an expert, and you have a chance of educating your client to "do it right."

The downside of the New Buy opportunity is that the Buying Center is complex and high level. Because of the risks involved in the purchase, lower level people tend to push decision making up, and high-level deciders tend to involve many influencers. In the worst case scenario, clients can become so anxious about the high risks inherent in the New Buy situation that they employ consultants to write an RFP and to make the short-list decision. From the seller's point of view, this turns the buying process into a crapshoot.

With a New Buy, the buying decision tends to lack stability. More simply, the decision maker may get "cold feet," delaying the purchase or going to a less risky alternative, probably a Modified Re-Buy. New Buys also tend to attract competition. They may start out as a sole-source opportunity, but expect the client to entertain other vendors.

# 11

# DEVELOPING A
# SALES STRATEGY

## YOU WANT THIS ONE!

Not all sales opportunities require heavy thought and strategy, but special prospects who fit your mission statement or marketing niche and provide great potential to develop full-service relationships merit special attention. And to apply special attention, you need help.

This chapter covers a great deal of ground. First, we will consider the value of, and a process for, involving others in sales strategies. Next, we will look at some strategy planning tools. Last, we will examine some ways to improve the probability of making the sale.

## DEFINING A SALES STRATEGY

A sales strategy is a plan for:

- Identifying members of the Buying Center.
- Influencing key members of the Buying Center to feel the needs and benefits.
- Defining what information you need to verify the need and the benefit.
- Overcoming the barriers to making the sale.
- Evaluating your current information and deciding what questions you still need to ask.
- Creating a plan for developing and testing your offering.
- Developing a plan for presenting your written proposal (engagement letter, etc.).

## CONDUCTING A STRATEGY REVIEW

Just as many professional firms use peer reviews to ensure the quality of their work, you need perspectives from others to develop or endorse your sales strategies. You may think that this suggestion would be "nice to do," but not very realistic. Once you try strategy review sessions, however, you will quickly recognize their benefits. Consulting firms that conduct such sessions find them enormously valuable.

Schedule two strategy review sessions for each major sales opportunity—the first right after you have successfully identified potential needs, and the second just before writing your proposal, engagement letter, or letter of agreement. Strategy Review 1 helps you to decide whether this prospect is worth pursuing and, if so, to create a plan for discovering obstacles. Strategy Review 2 helps develop a plan to give you a competitive advantage.

Invite four to six people to attend the session: members of your sales team and some colleagues who have no immediate knowledge of the prospect. Devote 60 to 90 minutes to the session. The person convening the session should provide a simple agenda:

1. Background information.
2. Sales Probability Index, assessing:
   • Type of Buy.
   • Need.
   • Prospect's Perception of Seller's Capabilities.
   • Highest Level of Influence.
   • Competition.
   • Overriding Client Goal.
3. Strategy development discussion.

## Who Can Afford the Time?

No one, of course, But that doesn't matter. If you are serious about business development, you'll make the extra effort. Furthermore, if you can institutionalize the process in your office, it will pay immense dividends. Selling professional services is a complex and difficult process requiring a constant source of fresh perspectives to help you come up with an effective strategy.

## STRATEGY REVIEW 1

### Sales Probability Index

Look at Figure 11.1 to get an idea of what the Sales Probability Index covers and how it is organized. The Index helps you make a point-in-time assessment of critical elements of the sales process, and helps you evaluate the probability of making the sale by assigning a point value to each element in the sales process. The higher the total score, the greater your probability of success.

The numerical value of the assessment poses some decisions. If it indicates a low probability, you may decide to develop

## SCORING

| | | | Score (Pts.) |
|---|---|---|---|
| A) | TYPE OF BUY | | |
| | Straight Re-Buy | 10 pts. | |
| | Modified Re-Buy | 6 | |
| | New Buy | 3 | _____ |
| | | | |
| B) | NEED | | |
| | Verified & Felt | 10 pts. | |
| | Verified & Not Felt | 6 | |
| | Presumed & Felt | 4 | |
| | Presumed & Not Felt | 0 | _____ |
| | | | |
| C) | BENEFIT | | |
| | Verifiable and Felt | 5 pts. | |
| | Expected and Felt | 3 | |
| | Verifiable or Expected and Not Felt | 1 | |
| | Not Verifiable, Expected and Felt | 0 | _____ |
| | | | |
| D) | PERCEPTION OF OUR FIRM'S CAPABILITIES | | |
| | Known & Positive | 10 pts. | |
| | Unknown/Neutral | 5 | |
| | Known & Negative | 0 | _____ |
| | | | |
| E) | HIGHEST LEVEL OF INFLUENCE | | |
| | Decision-Maker | 10 pts. | |
| | Influencer | 3 | |
| | Deduct 1 pt. if Decision-Maker is committee member. | | |
| | Add 2 pts. if Influencer is also a Ratifier. | | |
| | Add 2 pts. if Decision-Maker is also a User. | | |
| | (Total could exceed 10 pts.) | | _____ |
| | | | |
| F) | COMPETITION | | |
| | Sole Source | 10 pts. | |
| | 4 or Fewer Bidders | 5 | |
| | 5 or More Bidders | 2 | |
| | Note: If prospect is local, add 2 pts. | | |
| | If prospect is not local, subtract 2 pts. | | _____ |
| | | | |
| G) | BONUS | | |
| | Relating to Overriding Client Goal | 10 pts. | _____ |

_____ TOTAL SCORE

**Figure 11.1   Sales Probability Index**

RATING*
|  |  |  |  |
|---|---|---|---|
| 1–20 pts | No Probability | 36–42 | Good Probability |
| 21–30 | Low Probability | 43+ | High Probability |
| 31–35 | Moderate Prob. |  |  |

*Assuming competitive price.

## KEY DEFINITIONS

### TYPE OF BUY

Because you need to evaluate the degree of risk the purchase poses to the decision-maker, the focus is more on the **individual** than on the company.

- Straight Re-Buy: the decision-maker has bought this service before and is knowledgeable about expected deliverables/outcomes and customary workplans/schedules.
- Modified Re-Buy: the decision-maker has bought a similar service before, and expects to buy a modified version of that service. However, something has occurred which calls for a change in the application or specifications of the service.
- New Buy: the decision-maker has never bought this service before.

### HIGHEST LEVEL OF INFLUENCE

The focus is on the person to whom we are directing our sales efforts.

- Decision-maker: an individual or most influential member of a decision-making committee.
- Influencer: an advisor to the decider.
  —User: the person who uses the service or is directly affected by the service.
  —Ratifier: approves the decision.

### NEED

The focus is on how the Buying Center perceives the need.

- Verified Need: Accurate and complete data (too much or too little of something) verifies the need for the proposed service.
- Presumed Need: Qualitative indications that data exists which would verify the need for the proposed service.
- Felt Need: The Buying Center perceives the need as evidenced by their initiating contact and/or by citing consequences which make resolving the need urgent and important.
- Not Felt: The Buying Center either has either not acknowledged that the need exists, regardless of how obvious it is to others, or has evaluated it a low priority.

**Figure 11.1**   *(Continued)*

---

**BENEFIT**

The focus is on how the Buying Center perceives the benefit that your solution will provide.

- Verifiable Benefit: Measurement systems are in place to verify that something has increased or decreased.
- Felt Benefit: The Buying Center perceives that your solution will move them from an unacceptable current situation to a desire future situation.
- Expected Benefit: No specific measurement system to verify an increase or decrease, but the Buying Center believes that a benefit will accrue.

**PERCEPTION OF SELLER'S CAPABILITIES**

The focus is on the Decision Maker's evaluation of our capabilities.

- Known/Positive (direct): Decision-Maker has previously experienced our services and has made a positive evaluation of our capabilities.
- Known/Positive (associated): Decision-Maker has previously used our services, but not those directly related to the current need.
- Unknown/Neutral: Decision-Maker has little or no direct knowledge of our capabilities.
- Known/Negative: Decision-Maker has reservations about our capabilities or has had a negative past experience with the firm.

**COMPETITION**

The number of competing proposals (external and/or internal) which the Buying Center will evaluate.

---

**Figure 11.1**    *(Continued)*

a strategy to raise the category values. Or, you may decide that the probability is so low that it does not merit further investment in time. Some circumstances can make this a good decision. Exuberance, optimism, ambition, and greed can occasionally cause you to chase projects that don't deserve the investment.

I will take you through each element in the Index and then, at the end of this chapter, offer suggestions for improving the probability of a sale.

**Type of Buy.**    A Straight Re-Buy provides the most points because you should have little difficulty understanding exactly what the prospect wants to buy, and it's likely that the prospect thoroughly understands the need. Because the need and benefits are already well established, look for second order needs (service and work process needs).

The Modified Re-Buy adds complexity and difficulty because the Buying Center has broadened and you must clarify needs. Look to the User to tell you why a Straight Re-Buy is no longer acceptable.

The New Buy offers the greatest sales challenge and provides the most excitement. New Buy opportunities require investing considerable sales time and skill because the prospect must wrestle with a high-risk buying decision.

**Need.** If you can gather facts that establish the *current unacceptable situation* as having too much or too little of something, you will have verified the need. Then, if you can get the Buying Center to confirm the negative consequences of taking no action, you will know that the need is *felt.* If you are weak on the Verified Need, dig for facts; if you are weak on the Felt Need, sell the consequences of inaction. This assessment is particularly important if you plan to propose something different from the prospect's expressed need.

**Benefit.** Because most sales are driven by Needs, the benefit side of the Perfect Sales Equation is accorded lesser value. The Verifiable Benefit means that the systems are in place for measuring an increase or decrease in something, and the Felt Benefit means that the Buying Center agrees that the increase or decrease would produce a desired future situation.

**Perception of Seller's Capabilities.** A track record of success can be immensely valuable. This is not just conventional wisdom. Since you offer intangible services, you can only describe what you can do and promise that you will do it well, on time and on budget. Prospects who buy a professional service must trust that you will produce the desired benefit.

**Highest Level of Influence.** You reduce your sales probability if you cannot establish contact with the person who has

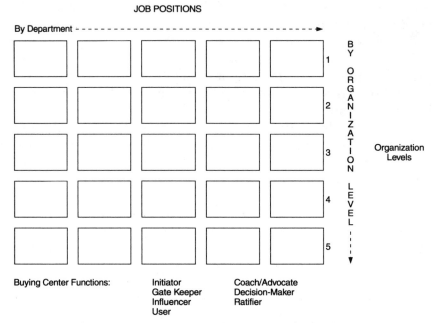

**JOB POSITIONS**

Figure 11.2    Buying Center Chart

the authority to make the buying decision. You should never feel comfortable relying on an influencer to do your selling for you.

Especially when soliciting a New Buy, plot all the members on an organizational chart (see Figure 11.2). In this way, you get an idea of the power relationships and a sense of who can influence whom on your behalf. Then, try to figure out where each member's self-interests lie, and how your offering will affect them personally. Determine who is in your camp, and who will oppose you.

You may note, for example, that your primary contact is two management levels below the decision maker, or in a different department or location. A regional or divisional person often initiates a project that has a corporate decision maker. In both cases, you must wonder how their lack of proximity to the decision maker will affect their ability to influence the buying decision. Knowing the relationships among the Buying Center members allows you to assess how much help you can expect from your initial contact.

Ultimately, you must decide how many members of the Buying Center you can see. Ideally, you will see them all, but because you are a part-time salesperson, you will seldom have the time to cover the entire membership.

**Competition.**   When a prospect entertains proposals from five or more firms, you must question the integrity of the buying process. Is this a shopping exercise? Is this an idea contest? Has the buyer done enough homework about qualified vendors, or is this a cattle call?

Case History

A few years ago, a Fortune 100 company sent more than 70 firms a request for proposals on a worldwide cash management study. To my knowledge, no one was awarded the assignment as described in the RFP. Eventually, the firm parceled out the work in smaller projects that never reached the originally proposed scope. The client apparently hadn't defined the scope and probable cost of the engagement, nor did it prequalify vendors. The combined cost of proposals from all the firms that decided to bid on all or part of the project probably exceeded a million dollars.

**Overriding Client Goal.**   Current CEO leadership techniques suggest focusing an organization on a certain goal such as changing its business strategy; concentrating on quality; or developing teamwork, accountability, or entrepreneurship. You'll find these goals proclaimed in executive memos, published in mission or strategy statements, or used as themes in management or sales conferences. When your prospect's organization has an overriding goal and that goal is shaping the actions of the firm's senior management, you may have found the keys to the vault—if you can associate your project with that goal. The Sales

Probability Index shows that you can earn a major competitive advantage with this bonus opportunity. It applies only if *you* have initiated the contact, or if you can *change the scope* of a client-initiated request for proposal.

When the CEO endorses an overriding goal, senior managers and department heads actively seek ways to demonstrate their support of that goal. Consequently, if you can bring a new idea or can suggest a modification of an existing program that promotes or sustains that goal, you will improve the probability of your sale substantially, and get your full billing rate as well.

Keep in mind that overriding corporate goals sometimes prompt a reorganization. You will find it extremely difficult to evaluate your sales probability during a reorganization because of the unpredictable political and psychological dynamics.

## Applying the Index

The Index indicates the strengths and weaknesses in your sales situation. You can then calculate the amount of time you will need to invest to improve the probability, and you will see clearly where you need to direct your efforts.

After thoughtful evaluation, you may decide to pursue a low probability prospect. I can think of three reasons:

1. The size and/or profitability of the job is too attractive to pass up.
2. You really want to do business with the client; this may be an opportunity to establish yourself.
3. You have nothing else to do.

A lot of professionals believe the second reason makes sense. I'm not so sure. They argue that submitting a proposal is a way of getting known and of positioning their firm for future consideration. True, you may get to know members of the Buying Center, but you if you do not get the work, you may become associated with failure.

## Index Validity

In a modest field test a few years ago, a client checked the validity of the Sales Probability Index with about 25 proposals. That, and my experience with the Index, indicate that the point scales work well enough. If you want to change the scales, however, go ahead, or change the Index in any way that makes it more useful to you. But, *use an index.* It forces you to ask some tough questions of yourself at a time when your optimism is at a high point.

## STRATEGY REVIEW 2

The first Strategy Review session helps you decide whether you should pursue this prospect. The second session helps develop a plan for improving the probability of success and for deciding whether you are ready to write a proposal or an engagement letter that will commit your offering to its final form.

### Improving Probability

The more obvious elements in the Index that can be improved are Need, Perception of Seller's Capabilities, and Highest Level of Influence. However, *all* elements can be improved.

**Type of Buy.**  New Buy situations often pose high risk, making the sale more difficult to consummate. Sometimes you can decrease the risk by reducing the scope of the engagement or by unbundling your proposal, beginning with a research, feasibility, or diagnostic stage. While these changes do not literally turn a New Buy into a Modified Re-Buy, they reduce the risk and, therefore, increase your probability of making the sale. So, go ahead and count the change as a Modified Re-Buy.

**Increasing the Need.**  If the need is not verified, you should collect facts that document the reality of the need. For example, many of the firm's area sales managers may feel entry level salaries are too low to attract high-quality candidates. No facts there, just opinions. How many area managers are dissatisfied? How many candidates have refused offers? What are the entry level salaries of firms attracting the quality candidates? You can argue that you should get paid for collecting such data, but if your competitor has done the digging and you haven't, who do you suppose will get the engagement?

Often, prospects won't let you into the organization to dig up the facts. In this case, construct some "best guess" numbers and ask Buying Center members how closely your data approximate their organization's situation. Then, you can adjust your figures whichever way will satisfy the Buying Center. Your goal is to get them to accept data as *sufficiently* complete, accurate, and relevant, and indicating that the current situation is unacceptable. Unless you have data to verify the need, you will be vulnerable to the question, "Why are we thinking of spending money on something we're not sure exists?"

When a Buying Center doesn't *feel* the need, that means that they aren't hurting. Their situation could be similar to what one cow said to another in the feeding pen next to the slaughterhouse: "Hey, we never had it so good!" Your job is to educate members on the negative consequences of maintaining the status quo.

If the Buying Center does not feel the need, try to quantify the cost of remaining in the current state. You may have to use "soft" numbers, such as the cost of *not* upgrading their management information system or the cost of letting a competitor build market share. Users stand to benefit most directly from your service, so try to convince them to become vocal advocates. Since the decision maker may be far removed from the problem and may not *feel* the need, look for data associated with the situation that affect corporate goals. To invest in a solution, your decision maker must believe that the current state is unacceptable.

**Creating a Verifiable Benefit.**    Some engagements provide the opportunity for easily measured benefits, such as decreasing response time or increasing profitability. Many don't, however, so you enable your prospect to envision a positive cost–benefit relationship without implying any guarantees.

Because a benefit describes a desired future situation, speculate on what that future situation might look like. Encourage your prospect to participate in this conjecture. Then, as you sell within the Buying Center, ask each member to confirm that achieving your "reasonable expectations" would in fact be desirable.

**Improving Perception of Capabilities.** In absence of a track record, try to produce an influential referral. Phone calls by your prospect to your standard list of references may not be enough—more often than not, prospects ask for references but never make the calls. So, maybe you can set up a meeting or a lunch with your prospect and a valued client because your client has had some related experiences he can share with your prospect. Provide examples of some deliverables from past engagements, anything that helps prove your capabilities.

You might reasonably ask why you would invest sales time when your prospect perceives your firm as "Known, Negative." Any professional service firm that has been around for a few years can probably cite an engagement that went sour, and to get future business from that prospect, you must earn the right to be considered again. Going through the sales process—even with virtually no probability of getting the work—allows the consultant to clear the air and rebuild the relationship.

**Competition.** In a tough competitive situation, you may need to do something dramatic to improve your probability of getting the business. One approach is to *change the playing field.* You may be able to improve your sales probability a great deal by proposing something different from the RFP's instructions or the prospect's directive. This attractive strategy gets your creative juices flowing and can produce wonderful results: It can reduce competition, expand the scope of the project, and allow you to value price. But, it can also be dangerous because you will be offering something other than what your prospect asked for. Your sense of optimism and enthusiasm may make you think your creative idea will "blow them away . . . ," but unless you do careful selling, the response is more likely to be, "Thanks, but that isn't what we asked for."

## Interrelationship of Competition and the Type of Buy

In terms of sales probability, Competition and Type of Buy are interrelated. For example, you can change a Straight Re-Buy into a Modified Re-Buy by finding additional needs. Although you lose points in the Index in that area, you may change the buy from competitive to sole source and, therefore, gain points.

### Case History

My company once responded to an RFP that asked for recommendations without organizational research. We did our preproposal selling and then submitted a proposal that included a research phase. The other three firms on the short list made firm recommendations without research. We reduced the number of competitors from three to one because the clients first had to decide the issue of research versus nonresearch.

While we won that one, we lost another with a similar tactic because we didn't know the Buying Center well enough to recognize that our proposal expanded the scope of the project. It moved the buy from Modified Re-Buy to New Buy, and the decision maker avoided a higher risk buy.

### Case History

A company has decided to implement a corporatewide total quality management (TQM) system and has requested a proposal from four qualified consulting firms—yours and three others. If you accept the expressed need/solution, you will interview the client to determine the scope of the project and then submit a proposal providing a price, work plan, and schedule, highlighting the "benefits" of working with your firm. (Remember, benefits are not benefits unless the client believes that they fill a need.) All the competitors, then, will have one chance in four of getting the work.

The client will compare "apples to apples" and select what appears to be the best (and least expensive) apple.

On the other hand, if you risk challenging the need/solution and conclude from your investigation that applying TQM to one small division first makes more sense than corporatewide, you may have good reason to propose a different solution. By doing so, you will have changed the competitive situation from comparing apples-to-apples to first comparing apples-to-an-orange (you're the orange), thus improving your competitive position substantially.

If the prospect prescribes the solution—turning the need into a requirement—then price can become a determining factor. The client can easily reason, "Because I am buying apples, and because apples are mostly the same, I'll have to give strong consideration to the least expensive apple." The "orange," then, has the option of value pricing.

## CHANGING THE SCOPE

As in the preceding examples, you may find reasons to change the scope of the project from the prospect's expressed need:

- You disagree with the prospect's assessment of the need.
- You believe that the implied solution to the expressed need is inappropriate.
- You have found some associated needs that your proposal will address.

However, before proposing something more or different from the prospect's request, you must find out what prompted your prospect's original direction to you. For example, was he:

- Directed by someone else?
- Acting out of ignorance?
- Looking for a low-cost solution, because of only a marginal need?
- Looking for a "quick fix" or temporary solution?

Understanding how the project was originally defined, will help you gauge the consequences of trying to change it.

Be sure that a verified and felt need anchors your proposed solution. And, remember that the prospect may "lose" something by giving up an expressed need. Try to figure out to what extent the expressed need is accepted throughout the Buying Center. It's almost impossible to overcome a Buying Center consensus even if your new approach is substantially better.

When you attempt to change the scope of a project, you will probably change the Buying Center as well. Expect new influencers, and possibly a new decision maker. Your strategy may, in fact, create major problems for your initiator, who may have been your greatest advocate. Chances are you will have made the buying situation more complex and the solution less "cut and dried." Conceivably, your proposed new scope could exceed the original decision maker's signing authority, therefore creating a new decision maker.

## REACHING THE DECISION MAKER

Because it makes no sense to sell to people who do not have the authority to buy, we need to explore this subject further.

Most everyone has difficulty in reaching those members of senior management who may be major influencers or decision makers. Often, the initiator acts as gatekeeper, restricting your contacts in the organization and keeping you on a "short leash." Sometimes senior management refuses to see vendors, delegating vendor contact to a lower level. And, quite commonly, less senior professionals feel uncomfortable trying to set up sales calls with senior management.

If the initiator tries to restrict your mobility within the organization, meet that head-on as soon as you can. At the end of your second visit, say, "I'll need to see X, Y, and Z, and I'd like to call them and get on their calendars." If the initiator objects, restate why you need to see these people and ask why he or she is opposed. Do not ask for permission to see people because that invites denial. Rather, state who you plan to see and then deal with the negative reaction if it comes.

If you must see the CEO, tell the initiator that you plan to call the CEO. Or, state that your firm has a policy for a senior member of your firm to call on senior management of the prospect's firm. Tell the initiator that you will not try to *sell* anything. Rather, you would like senior management's perspective as it might influence your project. If you or a senior member of your firm do see the CEO (or any other member of senior management), be sure to stick to "CEO talk," not "project talk." Discuss the future of the firm, the direction of the industry, competitive differentiation—whatever topics relate broadly to your project. *Do not* talk about the details of your project unless the CEO brings up the subject.

Even if senior managers have said they do not see vendors or consultants, chances are a senior member of your firm can reach them. Many sellers advise against "going over the client's head" because it will "alienate the client" and get you "thrown out of the office." That, in fact, may happen. But, more often, that predicted sequence provides an easy rationalization for not trying to reach the major influencers or decision makers.

Use your experience and your professionalism as leverage with the initiator by saying things such as:

> We need to talk to the VP-Marketing before we can make a valid recommendation.
>
> From past experience, we know we must get your President's input before we . . .
>
> It doesn't make any sense to go ahead without . . .

You can detect when the barriers are firm, and you should not push too hard, but at least, test the barriers.

As a final caution, keep in mind that a decision maker who is new to the job or to the organization may choose *not* to exert authority over the decision, especially if it is a New Buy.

## DEALING WITH GROUP MEMBERS WHO
## FEEL THREATENED

You must always keep in mind that someone in the client organization may find your services threatening. Look, first, among the technical influencers, then the political influencers. Then, spend some time with individuals who are likely to feel threatened. Under no circumstances should you avoid contact with those who feel threatened by your offering. Individuals who fear your services may do so because they don't understand exactly what you propose to do, how you propose to do it, and how it will affect them. Ignoring them only heightens their paranoia.

## TASK FORCES, BUYING COMMITTEES,
## AND ASSOCIATIONS

A senior executive who is part of a buying committee can be unpredictable in influencing the buy. Much depends on the executive's relationship with the committee and with the organization. If you don't know what the relationship is, don't guess. Ask more questions.

   Task forces are products of the new leadership concepts and are extraordinarily difficult to influence. In my opinion, they are risk-averse groups, that will always get proposals from more than one firm and will probably buy the solution or firm that offers the lower risk. They will buy a packaged solution before a custom-designed one, a well-known firm before one that is less known, a mid-range price before one that is high or low. Task forces often function like government bureaucracies, constructing senseless rules that limit the amount of contact they will permit before you submit a proposal, and regulating the amount of information they dispense to competing firms. They rationalize their approach as an effort to "be fair" to all involved. When selling to task forces, the consultant with an existing relationship has a major competitive advantage.

It's easy to think that the entire committee is the Buying Center. While technically it is, some members will have immensely more power and influence than others. Some members may even have the power to regulate what is brought to the committee and in what form it is delivered. You must discover those influences, and direct questioning may not get you the right answers. A good way to find out is to ask why and how the committee was constituted. Then, find out who's responsible for setting agenda and for facilitation. Chances are, that person has major influence. Ask if any outside or inside consultants advise the committee. They have power. Ask whom the consultants work with most of the time, outside of committee meetings. That may be another source of power.

## CONCLUSION

You will be amazed at how much you will learn from Strategy Review sessions and what effective strategies you can develop. Many professionals give little thought to strategy. They plow ahead and hope to win the job with a great proposal or a deeply discounted price. A great proposal cannot overcome a bad job of selling, however, nor can you write a great proposal unless you've done a good job of selling. And, discounted pricing—just to get you in the door—seldom produces a mutually satisfying relationship.

# 12

# WORKING YOUR STRATEGY

This first part of this chapter will explore working your strategy in a prospect-initiated opportunity. The second part will explore an approach to use when you discover the opportunity.

## WORKING YOUR STRATEGY WHEN THE PROSPECT HAS CALLED YOU

### Responding to the Expressed Need

The prospect invited you to discuss a project and described a need. However, as mentioned earlier, the expressed need may have been a solution. Or, because of your greater experience, you saw the expressed need as a symptom not the root cause of the problem. In that first call, you made some cursory attempts at qualifying that need but did not challenge the prospect's thinking because, at this point in your relationship, you do not have the trust or credibility to try to function as an expert when the prospect is probably looking for an implementer.

Back in your office, your strategy review prior to your second meeting helped you recognize that you have reached a critical stage in the sales process. After this call, you must make some important decisions about *how* you will proceed, or *if* you will proceed. Because business development is so expensive in terms of the time it takes, you must be willing to walk away from something with a low probability of success.

If you sense that the Expressed Need is carved in stone, then to get the assignment, you must accept the role of implementer. Do you want to? Can you afford not to? Can you believe that the prospect's solution will resolve the need? What happens if your prospect asks you to propose on an engagement that you think won't solve the real problem? Do you want to try to change the scope of the engagement, or change the engagement altogether?

Let's look at a real case.

### Case History

The company, an avionic manufacturer with annual sales of approximately $20 million, was founded 30 years ago by two engineers; they are currently the president and the vice president of sales and marketing. The company manufactures parts for original equipment manufacturers (OEMs) such as Cessna and Beech as well as the U.S. government. The company produces stock parts as well as custom orders.

A management consulting firm was selected, noncompetitively, to perform an inventory management study. The engagement was recommended to the president by the chief financial officer. Both the CFO and the company's lead bank had concerns about the high level of inventory. The president, however, asserted that inventory levels were not excessive. He asked the consultants to make recommendations to reduce production delays and frequent part shortages by improving inventory management practices. Now, the consultants would like to submit a proposal to help implement the recommendations from their initial study.

At the conclusion of the initial engagement, the consultants tried unsuccessfully to schedule a meeting to present their recommendations to top management. Instead, the president requested a written report that he subsequently sent to the bank. Apparently, the president used the consultant's report only to allay the bank's concerns. He showed no interest in pursuing the consultants' recommendations.

## What Went Wrong?

In this sales effort, the Expressed Need and the resulting engagement (solution) didn't match. The bank and the CFO felt that inventory levels were too high, but the president did not. Instead, he wanted recommendations for improving inventory management practices, which could be ignored or implemented as he wished. Without knowing what data were used by the bank and CFO to *verify* the need, we know for certain that the president did not *feel* the need. Perhaps the president didn't understand the consequences of the excess inventory, or he may have understood the consequences but felt a large inventory was necessary to provide excellent customer service. So, the consultants played an implementer role and served the president's interest of pacifying the bank and the CFO. Presumably, the consultants knew that the engagement didn't match the need, but they rationalized that undoubtedly there were problems in the client's inventory management practices that they could solve. Then, once they had established the relationship, they could deal with the larger problem: excess inventory. They apparently decided it was better to get the work than to try to change the scope of the assignment.

## Pros and Cons of Changing the Scope

Consultants frequently look for ways to change the scope of the Expressed Need engagement. As discussed in the last chapter, this is sometimes a good sales strategy because it can provide the opportunity for you to increase fees and to function in an expert role. More often, however, it is problematic. You should consider changing or expanding the scope in the following situations:

- The competition is formidable (better known, established relationship, or just sheer numbers).
- The engagement is unreasonably price sensitive.

Before deciding to change or expand the scope, be sure that:

- The buying center does not change.
- The organizational environment is relatively stable.
- You have direct contact and mutual understanding with the decision maker.

In the preceding case, the consultants did not have a mutual understanding with the president, the decision maker. If they had developed a working relationship, they could have tried to persuade him to change the scope of the assignment (using the strategy model cited in Chapter 4). And, even if they had failed, they at least would have learned the president's interests and might have found some way to accommodate both his concerns and the real needs of his company.

## Applying the Sales Probability Index

Whether you respond to the Expressed Need or decide to change the scope, the Sales Probability Index that you completed in your strategy session indicates what information you still need to gather. Also, on subsequent calls don't be afraid to revisit topics you discussed on your first call. You'll be surprised how often you will get different answers to the same questions.

Your conversations should involve nine topics that can be organized into two major parts: the Job and the Buy:

*The Job*

1. Scoping the project.
2. Solving the Perfect Sales Equation.
3. The budget.
4. The due date.

*The Buy*

5. The Type of Buy.
6. The Buying Center.

7. The buying decision process.
8. The buying decision or selection criteria.
9. Competition.

## Objectives

Your primary objective in your next call is to cover the job-related topics: scoping the job, solving the unknowns in the Perfect Sales Equation (at least as interpreted by the initiator), and determining if this is a "real" project, meaning that there should be a firm budget and a due date. Your secondary objectives are related to the buy: the type, the Buying Center, the buying criteria and process, and the nature of your competition.

It's tempting to try to accomplish both the job and the buy objectives in one call because all the aspects are interrelated. However, the more calls you make (within reason), the more opportunities you have to build a relationship. Furthermore, covering just the job-related objectives thoroughly will take a lot of time. Therefore, you should ask your prospect for at least an hour and a half, and hope you can stretch it into two. If you can't get an hour and a half, you should begin to wonder about the seriousness of the project or of the initiator's interest in you as a candidate. Prospects often need second and third bids to create the illusion of an open competition, and I have found that if the prospect will not invest time with me, the assignment is probably a "lock" for someone else.

**Scoping the Project.**   In your initial contact, your prospect described the proposed assignment, but you didn't get enough information. If you have used a strategy session properly, you will now be armed with a range of questions that will allow you to confirm what you understood was the situation and to clarify details. So, even though it may be somewhat repetitious, listen carefully while your prospect redescribes the project and be prepared to unpack some of the information. Get definitions of abstract terms such as "urgency," "more responsive," or "team building." You need absolute clarity here.

Be sure you understand the description of the deliverables; compare them with the goals and make sure they match. Client expectations often change as the project progresses, and you need a baseline to justify billing for client-initiated changes.

**Solving the Perfect Sales Equation.**  As you discuss the scope of the project, you can also begin solving the Perfect Sales Equation. You can start anywhere in the equation; the best place is where your prospect leads you. In the prospect-initiated call, that will probably be the *expressed need*. You can presume that expressing the need means the prospect, or someone senior to him or her, feels the current situation is unacceptable. Check it out. Start with a question about the priority of the project. "How important is this project? Is this a top priority for your department?"

Then, try to verify the need with a few questions:

How did you first recognize that something had to be done? So, would it be correct to say that you determined that you had too much [too little] of . . . ? How do you know that for sure? Are there data to support your contention? What *specifically* does your current system fail to do?

Next, work with the solution part of the equation:

You've said that you want to schedule a management retreat . . . have you thought of any other way at getting at the problem?

Then, go to the Verifiable Benefit:

So, presuming that we organized and facilitated this management retreat, what would success look like? If all we did was increase the mutual awareness of problems in these areas, do you think that would be enough?

Then, to the Felt Benefit:

Would everybody be satisfied if you accomplished that, or are you just speaking for yourself?

Then, back to the Felt Need:

What would happen if we didn't do anything for another six months? What would be the consequences?

It's appropriate to skip around the equation; it keeps the conversation lively, and varying the questions tends to produce more thoughtful answers. And, you now have a foundation to talk money again.

**The Budget.**  Many professionals are uncomfortable asking about budgets or giving prices. If you have this problem, you must overcome it. The less direct you are about money and the longer you delay discussing it, the more difficulties you will create for yourself and for your prospect.

If your prospect specified a budget on your first call that seems insufficient, bring up the subject again. Coming on the heels of a discussion of needs and benefits, the budget may have grown somewhat. If you have serious concerns about the realism of the budget, voice them now in terms of needs and benefits. Say something like this: "You've described a very serious problem, and you are looking for a significant improvement. But, frankly, I don't think you're planning to put enough money behind this project to ensure success."

**The Due Date.**  Whereas learning how much money the prospect is willing to spend helps you decide how much you're willing to invest, the existence of a due date probably means that someone thinks the project is important. If your prospect says, "We definitely want to get started on this late next quarter," you have a good clue that this may not be a real project yet. More likely, the prospect is just "picking a few brains." Be responsive, but don't invest a lot of time until the due date becomes firm.

## Follow-Up Call to Discuss the Buy

If you require another call to cover buy-related topics, you can easily consume another 90 minutes. When you begin the call, you should reconfirm any critical information you gathered earlier, because in the interim, conditions affecting the assignment may have changed, and the prospect may have forgotten to update your data. So, start out with the question, "What's changed since we last talked?" Then briefly summarize the key issues and ask your prospect to confirm that you are on target.

**Type of Buy.**    A simple question such as, "What kind of experience have you or your company had with projects such as this?" will confirm the type of buy. Be most concerned about New Buy situations. Unless the proposed project is small or its impact can be contained within a small group, look for a high-level decision maker in New Buy situations and be extremely skeptical if your prospect tells you differently. If it is a New Buy, be prepared to invest a lot of time educating and counseling your prospect.

**Buying Center.**    The conversation regarding the type of buy leads easily into the Buying Center discussion. At this call, you must set in motion your plan to schedule meetings with the other members of the Buying Center. If necessary, you must be tenacious and overcome resistance. If you doubt your ability to come up with good reasons for meeting with others, write out reasons ahead of time and rehearse what you will say. For example, be ready to counter a resistance such as "They won't see you," or "I think I'll be able to answer all your questions."

Asking permission to see other members of the Buying Center does not work as well as stating that you need to talk to these people. If you encounter resistance, tell your prospect that your past experience has made it clear that you must see certain key people. In a competitive situation, and without a current relationship with the client, it may be extremely difficult to get to high-level influencers or the decision maker, but you must try.

Getting to the key members of the Buying Center is hard and time-consuming work. You will be able to rationalize many reasons, in this particular situation, for not needing to see others or for it being impossible to see others. I have heard all the reasons before and have used most of them myself. And, every time I fail to meet with other members of the Buying Center, I regret it.

**The Buying Process.** Ask your prospect to take you, step by step, through the buying decision process. Then, try to figure out how you can participate in each step. Are you needed to answer difficult questions? Do "they" need to meet you to have faith in the project? If yours is a sole-source proposal, odds are that you can be a part of the process. If you are responding to a request for proposal, the best you can do is get short-listed for an interview.

**Buying and Selection Criteria.** This is a wonderful topic of conversation because it can expose a prospective client's decision-making weaknesses and give you an opportunity to exert influence. Ask questions such as "How will you evaluate our proposal?" or "You have asked some excellent firms to submit proposals, so how will you differentiate among us?" Your prospect is likely to give some abstract answers and to minimize the role of price in the buying decision.

Just as with any other abstract answer you get, you must unpack criteria statements and clarify your prospect's definition. Also, look for hidden inferences behind some criteria. Location is a criterion that often comes up, conventional wisdom inferring that the closer you are to the client, the better and cheaper service you can provide. Distance, however, is not the only measure of good and inexpensive service.

If you detect that your prospect is starting to feel embarrassed from a lack of well-defined criteria, offer your own. You can say something like, "For what it's worth, I can give you a list of criteria that we have collected over the years that has served buyers of our types of services quite well." Then, send a copy of the list on plain, white paper, with no company identification. Make your list as easy to photocopy as possible, and you'll be surprised how often it is used.

When your prospect says "price is very important," simply ask why. If the answer is direct and specific, and given without hesitancy, you should probably believe it. If your question catches the prospect by surprise, or if you sense that he or she is ad-libbing, then the person is probably trying to scare you into a low bid. At this point, since there is nothing you can relate the price position to, it won't do you any good to challenge it. So, regardless of the answer, immediately shift the conversation to, "What else is important besides price?"

**Competition.** Knowing about competition may not be as important as knowing about budget, but you can learn some important information. For example, a prospect who claims to be talking to 10 firms:

1. May not be very knowledgeable about buying from professional firms.
2. May not have a good understanding of the need and is looking for ideas.
3. May be price shopping.

If the prospect is just talking to two firms, you should find out why yours was selected. You should also know who you will compete against. For example, if you are with a major firm, and your competitors are all small firms, you should ask why your prospect is talking to such a wide variety of firms. Sometimes, if you know your competition well, you can predict what strengths they may emphasize or approach they may propose, and you can figure out some competitive advantages.

## Meeting with the Buying Center

This stage in the sale presents many situational variables. In most cases, however, you will now meet with members of the Buying Center. In doing so, you must use essentially the same approach used with the initiator. Your purpose is to corroborate what you have already learned, or to identify the differences. Therefore, you must explore carefully each aspect of the Perfect Sales Equation except the solution, which presumably you have not yet developed.

Some people hurry through these interviews as if their sole purpose is to identify advocates and adversaries. In reality, however, whatever evidence you gather to identify advocates or adversaries is probably inconclusive. Each member of the Buying Center has his or her interests in the project and will probably describe these interests in exaggerated ways to make a strong impression on you since you are being considered as someone who can "fix" the problem. So, people who initially appear to be adversaries may just be strong proponents of their own interests. Furthermore, because you are providing an intangible service and must use abstract language to describe its dimensions and conditions, the probability of initial misunderstanding is enormous. Before counting someone as an adversary, try to keep Dr. Kenneth Johnson's words in mind: "We must expect to be misunderstood. We must expect to misunderstand."

A further complication is that at this point, you are extremely knowledgeable about the situation, and the people in the Buying Center may be barely up to speed. In addition, many professional assignments involve some organizational change, which some people welcome and others find extremely threatening. So, take your time in these interviews. Listen carefully. And, explore the needs and benefits sides of the Perfect Sales Equation.

## WORKING YOUR STRATEGY WHEN YOU HAVE SOLICITED THE PROSPECT

Although selling to an opportunity that you have created is far more difficult than selling to an opportunity defined by the prospect, the rewards can be great. If you are successful, chances are it will be a noncompetitive buy and you will have established yourself in an expert role.

### Apparent Needs Are Fragile—Handle with Care

In your initial call, let's presume that you either uncovered an apparent need or you hooked your prospect on a good idea. You are probably feeling optimistic, and eager to move ahead. What's more, you expect that your prospect feels much the same way. On the latter point, you are probably wrong. In general:

1. The prospect doesn't remember as much about your first discussion as you do.
2. Whatever your prospect's reactions at the first meeting, they've changed.
3. You read into the project more interest than your prospect actually feels.
4. You feel much more urgency about the project than your prospect does.

Therefore, the first objective of this call is to rekindle your prospect's interest. You can do so by encouraging your prospect to disclose the opinions that he or she formed at your first call. How did your ideas "settle in"? Did your prospect get caught up in the excitement of a new idea only to cool down later? After giving the idea more thought, did he or she become overwhelmed with the complexity of the problem or need and lose appetite for trying to find a solution? Was your prospect responding with polite enthusiasm to show appreciation for your interest and effort?

Although you must get answers to the preceding questions, you would pose an interpersonal confrontation by asking them directly. So, begin the call by showing your prospect something that will re-establish his interest. It might be a published article, a study, a paper you wrote—anything that gets your prospect back up to speed and refocuses attention on the situation that you discussed. Then, ask the prospect to respond. The following dialogue illustrates this point.

> Stan, thinking about our conversation last week, I thought you might be interested in this report, which pretty well parallels the issues we discussed. For example, take a look at . . .

You might conclude this part of your discussion by saying, "So, as I reflected on what we discussed, I felt very positive. But, bring me up to date—what's your current thinking?"

Be prepared for your prospect to say he or she hasn't thought much about it, or to raise some objection. This could mean:

- The prospect does not see the issue as high urgency and does not have a felt need, meaning that you must provide a convincing argument for the negative consequences of doing nothing.
- The issue may not fall within the prospect's job responsibility, therefore you must find out with whom the responsibility lies.
- The prospect may not believe there will be a personal reward for initiating action on this issue, therefore, you must learn more about your prospect, *personally.*

Lots of ideas seem great at inception and lose their luster as time passes. Be prepared for that to happen with yours. As a way of building credibility *and* creating a felt need, consider an approach such as this:

> I've been giving some thought, Pat, to our discussion last week, and I had to consider, with everything else on your plate, why would you make this a high-priority project? So, I've developed this scenario that tries to identify the consequences of the situation and poses the question, what would happen if you did nothing? I'd like to know how closely my scenario matches the real situation.

One approach for building your scenario is to take the data that verify the need and project it into the future. If the need is real, its consequences should multiply as you project into the future. Another approach is to identify the "ripple effect" of a problem, showing how far-reaching the problem really is.

If you have successfully rekindled your prospect's interest, start to work the benefit side of the Perfect Sales Equation. People can sometimes repress obvious needs because they can't envision the future desired situation. So, help your prospect see how his or her world would look with the need removed.

As a professional, you can take an organizational view of the need situation. Your prospect, however, will probably look at issues very personally and will evaluate your idea on "what's in it for me?" You will never make a serious error in judgment if you expect your prospects and clients to make decisions based on personal rather than organizational consequences.

Next, try to figure out how your prospect can personally benefit from promoting your proposed idea. A prospect who cannot detect a personal reward will lose interest in the project: Most people have plenty to do and select their activities based on what they *must* do, what they *like* to do, and what will bring them *rewards*.

It may turn out that your idea was interesting to your prospect but that its application will not produce any personal reward. This is only a minor setback. Your prospect can tell you *who* in the organization will benefit personally from your idea and, therefore, will be most likely to respond to your sales attention.

## Offer a Presentation

If your prospect has cooled to the apparent need or your idea, consider offering to put on a presentation for interested parties. The true nature of this should be educational, for example, new concepts in total quality management, or current trends in managing diversity or sexual harassment, whatever is the knowledge specialty of your practice. Then, prepare the most interesting and substantive educational presentation you can. Completely ignore, for the time, any idea of turning this into a sales event. You have two objectives with this presentation: (1) to build awareness of a need among a potential buying center, and (2) to establish yourself as valued resource. Go back to Chapter 7 and reread the paragraphs on establishing yourself as competent, credible, and compatible. If you can schedule a presentation, you will have a wonderful opportunity to demonstrate all three qualities.

You also have the possibility of destroying your opportunity for business, maybe forever. Presentations can make strong impressions—either positive or negative—on many people. You will destroy your opportunity for business if your audience perceives your presentation as irrelevant, superficial, or a sales ploy.

Your presentation will be irrelevant if you have not done careful research on your prospect, superficial if you put new cosmetics on old information, or a sales ploy if you "toot your own horn" by citing successful engagements with "name" clients.

This is one presentation that you must rehearse regardless of your talent as a presenter. The purpose of the rehearsal is to allow an objective audience to judge whether your presentation is relevant, substantial, and strictly educational. You can't be a good judge of your own material.

The only "sell" you should consider putting in such a presentation should be positioned at the end. If you have planned time for a discussion, you can begin by voicing your hope that the presentation might suggest some areas where you could be a valued resource and then let your audience pick up the discussion if they will. (If you are five minutes from your allotted time, it is not likely you will generate discussion, so unless you have developed a great deal of interest, don't try.) If your presentation has been relevant, substantial, and free from self-promoting elements, suggesting a discussion will not offend and may, in fact, open a high-potential opportunity.

## SUMMARY

Having made it through the "preliminaries" of the sales process, you now have new and better information for making an objective evaluation of your sales opportunity. Use the Perfect Sales Equation to help you make that important judgment. Look at the four unknowns (verified and felt needs, verifiable and felt benefits) and assess to what extent you have solved those unknowns. Your assessment will give you a benchmark from which to reshape your sales strategy:

1. Create a strategy to solve each unknown in the Perfect Sales Equation.
2. Learn who can fund the project.
3. Negotiate a due date.

**4.** Ask about competition (look for in-house).

**5.** Define the type of buy.

**6.** Identify the Buying Center.

**7.** Identify how they will make the buying decision.

From this point on, the prospect-initiated opportunity and the consultant-initiated opportunity follow the same path to closure except for the request for proposal, which I will discuss separately.

# 13

# PRESENTING THE "WHAT IF" PROPOSAL

All along, you've talked needs and benefits and have spent very little time discussing your approach to the service you're going to provide. What's more, you may have known what you were going to propose by the end of the first call, but only now do you get to unholster the stuff you are famous for—a good, thoughtful approach to the prospect's problem.

The best business developers I know do the following two things better than their less successful colleagues:

1. They delay discussing their solution until they have tested the needs and benefits with the key members of the Buying Center.
2. They delay writing a proposal until they have tested their proposed offering with the key members of the Buying Center.

## MEETING WITH MEMBERS OF BUYING CENTER

Anything you propose must get the endorsement of most if not all the members of the Buying Center. They cannot endorse a solution, however, if they don't agree on the needs and benefits. The time-consuming task of meeting with key members of the Buying Center may tempt you to take shortcuts, but the best business developers don't. Instead, they try to present a "what if" proposal to each key member, including the decision maker.

Successful business developers also know that *until* they have committed their approach to writing, they can make whatever changes the Buying Center members deem necessary. Their final proposal will then have no surprises and will reflect everyone's previously agreed-to terms.

### But They Want a Proposal!

Inexperienced business developers sometimes offer prematurely to write a proposal, and their prospects, not surprisingly, agree to look at it. Other times, prospects request a proposal at the end of the first call. Cynical as it may sound, prospects know that a good way of getting rid of you is to let you submit a proposal or to ask you to write a proposal and then turn it down. At best, they may have shown a mild interest; and at worst, they're being deviously polite. Sadly, when you submit a proposal that is untested and off the mark, you will have proven conclusively to the Buying Center that you do not understand their needs. You won't get the work and you will have probably damaged your chances for future business. So, when it's time to present your solution, use the "what if" proposal technique instead.

### Advantages of the "What If?" Proposal

Describing your approach by using "what if" questions provides at least three advantages: It encourages your prospect (1) to focus, (2) to evaluate, and (3) to contribute. If you use the process appropriately, you will stimulate some objections that you have the time and opportunity to handle.

Some prospects have the frustrating habit of neither listening carefully nor evaluating critically what you say until they "see something in writing." They say things such as, "Write it up and let me take a look at it." At this point in the sales process, putting something in writing is the last thing you should do, but on the other hand, you can't afford to let your client delay paying attention any longer. You must make the prospect grapple with the same issues that you grapple with.

## Build a "Strawman"

One technique for focusing a client is to present what you can call a "strawman" but, in reality, is exactly what you intend to propose. The strawman label invites your prospect to offer criticism, and, because you have used an oral presentation, your prospect cannot give you a conclusive "no." When describing your solution and work plan, use (as often as you can without sounding ridiculously repetitive) questions starting with "what if". Rather than saying, "We recommend that we spend a couple of weeks . . . ," say:

> What if we spent a couple of weeks in the field with some of your better salespeople and observed them making customer calls on some of those companies you have targeted for "partnering?"

Responses to "what if" questions will give you insights into a prospect's self-interests and understanding of the situation. You will be surprised at how often a strawman brings out new information or evidence of misunderstandings even after long discussions with your prospect have led you to believe you were in accord.

## Group Presentations

Ideally, you will make "what if" proposals one-on-one to key members of the Buying Center and then will follow those meetings with the formality of presenting your written proposal or engagement letter. The proposal presentation should confirm to the group what you have already sold individually. When you cannot have a separate meeting with each key member, you will have to make a "what if" group presentation. This is *not* just a formality to confirm the buy, this is a group selling event to co-alesce all the different interests and ideas and gain consensus. Not an easy job.

The "what if" presentation should differ from the conventional format, which is a monologue followed by questions and answers. Rather, it should be a controlled dialogue in which you elicit critical evaluation after each point in your agenda. In this way, you can get the feedback you need, when you need it, and can control the sequence of information.

If you predict that your Buying Center won't readily give you such feedback, prepare to pause and ask direct and specific questions. You should ask:

> How does this plan compare with . . . . ?
>
> Who's going to feel threatened if we start digging into . . . ?
>
> Give me your reaction to our price.
>
> I suspect that our approach is different from what you have been hearing from _____ . . .
>
> What are the soft spots in this approach?

You must ferret out all the objections because you still have the time to explain or resolve misunderstandings or disagreements. If you leave objections below the surface, you may never have a chance to resolve them, and they will damage you. If your prospects seem reluctant to make meaningful comments, which can happen in a group setting, use this appeal:

> I need your feedback. We have identical interests. You want a proposal that exactly meets your needs; I want to give you a proposal that exactly meets your needs. If I give you a proposal that misses your needs, it's worthless to both of us. My guess is that the proposal I've outlined falls short of meeting all your needs. So, tell me where it falls short.

Many professionals lose their professional objectivity when members of the Buying Center come up with good ideas during their "what if" presentations. This is not surprising, because it's difficult to recognize someone else's good idea when you're trying to sell your own. It's hard to be a good listener when you're trying to be a good presenter.

You must avoid behaving defensively when someone misunderstands, offers criticism, or makes suggestions. You have been working with this sale for a long time, *you* understand your recommendation completely, but they may not; and *you* are convinced that you can make it work, on time, and on budget, but they're not. Some Buying Center members may be hearing your recommendation for the first time, and they need to voice their concerns. I have observed "what if" presentations where the presenter actually trampled a prospect's idea or dismissed it by saying, "OK, if you could just hold that thought, I think you'll see why we recommend that . . ."

Even though your prospect's suggestions seem inappropriate, or not carefully thought out, you must listen carefully. The idea itself may not be on target, but it may indicate some underlying dissatisfaction with or misunderstanding of what you have presented. If someone's suggestion captures the interest of the audience, do not try to defeat it or incorporate it into your solution. I have never seen anyone who can think that quickly and cleverly. *So, stop your presentation.* Acknowledge that the suggestion deserves careful attention. Get the group to set up a subcommittee to evaluate the suggestion and get yourself on that committee. This recommendation is difficult to put into practice: Almost everyone I have observed in this predicament continues the presentation and tries to orchestrate some spontaneous resolution to the situation, invariably creating a host of downstream problems—far more than those involved in stopping the presentation.

## Presentation Sequence

All "what if" one-on-one meetings or group presentations must begin with a review of your understanding of the prospect's needs. You must check to see:

**1.** If everyone still agrees with the needs,

**2.** If anything has changed that might affect the needs.

Also, this quick discussion reconfirms the needs and "tunes up" the group to be receptive to your approach. Then, follow the sequence shown in Table 13.1. Most steps in your presentation are followed by feedback. Do *not* ask your group to hold their questions. Your objective is to get your prospect's oral endorsement of your approach, not to complete your presentation on time.

In almost every presentation I have observed, the consultants discuss the price at the very end. In my opinion, that makes absolutely no sense unless you are coming in with a price so low that your audience will rise up en masse and applaud. In all other cases, talk dollars first.

**Table 13.1   Oral Proposal—Process Model**

| Consultant | Prospective Client |
| --- | --- |
| States price and reviews evidence of verified need; Asks: What has changed? | Agrees that verified need exists |
| Reviews opinions that current situation is unacceptable | Agrees that current situation is unacceptable |
| Confirms that prospect has authority and funds to take action | |
| Recommends a future situation (benefits) | Agrees that future situation is desirable |
| Recommends (proposal) an offering (features) to produce desired situation (benefits); relates features/benefits to price. | Agrees that offering (features) will produce desired situation (benefits); comments on price. |
| Confirms next step | |

A common reaction to this suggestion is that if you bring up price first, you'll probably scare your prospects and they won't hear anything else you say. Well, if your price is *that* high, yes, you will scare them. But, try this technique: State your price and then say something like, "Our estimated price for this project is $XXX, which, I suspect, is higher than you expected. I wouldn't be here, however, unless I felt I could justify the reasons for that budget, and I'd like you to keep that in mind as we go through our presentation." That approach will capture their attention, not lose it. Also, you can tell them you will disclose the details of your price later in the presentation.

Look at the effects of discussing price at the end. First of all, you look much more confident if you fearlessly state your price at the beginning instead of waiting until the very end. But most important, if you do a superb job of describing the wonderful things you will do for your prospect, your listeners have to wonder how much all this will cost. Then, with five minutes left in the presentation, you tell them your price. Now, to justify your price, they must have perfect recall of everything you have said, and if they don't, you have only five minutes to justify it. Chances are pretty good that you will end your presentation on a sour note—a high price, insufficiently justified.

## Presentation Techniques

- Bring very little in writing to the presentation, probably only a discussion outline and a few exhibits. If you bring a draft of your proposal, you may be tempted to leave it, saying, "Now, we all know there are things in here that we have to correct, so please don't base your decision on this document . . ."
- Do not defend your offering with "yes, but." Treat all objections as valid. Encourage your prospect to explain the objection fully before you respond.
- If, even after you have tried to justify your price, your prospect has serious price objections, first review the verified and felt need, then discuss unbundling your service or reducing the scope. See Appendix B for a more complete discussion of price objections.

- If you run past your allotted time, say so, and ask for more time or for another meeting to finish the process. Do *not* rush to finish by eliminating feedback opportunities.

## CLOSURE

There are no magic closes. If you have done a good job of selling, the close is a natural extension of your oral proposal. You can't wait for your prospect to offer you the project, so you must ask some closing questions, such as:

> What haven't we covered? What needs to be done before we can do business together?
>
> Does our approach meet every one of your needs?
>
> If I summarize this in an engagement letter or a written proposal, do we have the business?

Because of the nature of the group (some presold, some not up to speed), you probably will need to use a conditional close. That is, you will not get a complete approval because of some unresolved details (conditions). In phrasing a conditional close, summarize what you have agreed on and then cite those issues that still need resolution. You can say, "We have agreed on most of the major issues, but have still to resolve _____ and _____. If we can satisfy you on those issues, may I assume that we have a deal?"

If you used a conditional close and need to correct your approach, schedule another presentation *before* you leave the room. If all you need is to confirm your approach in writing, schedule a time to deliver your proposal.

Case History "What If" Presentation

The business manager of a small liberal arts college—a long-term, occasional client—came to the consultants' office for a demonstration of a computer system, Solomon III. During the meeting, all agreed that Solomon III was inadequate and that the college needed a larger, multiuser system to integrate the business office, financial aid, registration, and fund-raising activities. The business manager disclosed at the meeting that the college lacked the funds to study and select the proper system.

In follow-up telephone conversations over a four-month period, the consultants learned that the college had contracted to buy a Data General computer system. The consultants successfully sold a small engagement to review the software documentation and determine the software's "fit and finish" for use by the college. With as much confidence as can be gained from reading manuals, the consultants declared the software a "qualified fit" and registered their technical and procedural concerns. The college expressed satisfaction with the engagement and said it would implement the consultants' recommendation for further research into specific features and functions.

The college had not appointed anyone to project-manage the installation of the multiuser system, apparently waiting for one of the users to step up to the responsibility. None had, each claiming the additional responsibility would take up too much time. Furthermore, the $100,000 price of the hard/software had tapped the college's budget. One user, the Vice President of Academic Affairs, who advocated hiring an overall project manager, suggested the consultants as being ideal for that role and asked them to write a proposal.

The consultants, who were able to graciously decline writing a proposal, instead scheduled an appointment with the college president to make a "what if" presentation. One of the consultants began:

As you know, we were asked to submit a proposal for how we might function as the overall project manager to oversee the installation of your new computer system. We felt it was premature for us to put anything in writing and wanted, instead, to meet with you, run through how we might approach such an assignment, and get your opinions on what makes sense and what doesn't.

[Turning to a flip chart] "First of all," we expect this to be a 9- to 12-month project, and we estimate our fees at

$3,000 to $4,000 per month. We think that the most this project would cost is $48,000, and if it goes without a hitch, our fees would be closer to $30,000. I'll get into the details of how we have arrived at our fees later on, but we believe that our purpose for this meeting is to discuss whether this expenditure makes good economic sense.

The consultants then went on to confirm that none of the users had volunteered to take on the project manager role. They asked, "What if you selected one of them, temporarily took him or her off regular duties, and gave that person project management responsibility?" The president responded that he had thought of that but wondered if anyone had the skills to manage the project; he also felt that none of them had sufficient backup to cover the regular duties. The discussion concluded that the college had no one internally who could manage the project and that Data General wouldn't be an appropriate choice. The consultants continued:

While everyone seems to agree that an overall project manager is needed, we thought it would be important to outline exactly what we think a project manager would contribute, and see if this is what you, too, have in mind.

At this point, the consultants had received confirmation that there was a Verified Need: that the college had no internal resources to manage the project. To pull out the Felt Needs, they offered a "strawman" showing what a project manager might contribute. The purpose of this tactic was to prompt the president's opinion; the consultants hoped for his concurrence that a project manager's contribution would, in fact, provide needed value, that (following the Perfect Sales Equation) the absence of project management represented an unacceptable situation.

Continuing with the presentation, in building their "strawman," the consultants listed the functions of a project manager on the flip chart, then turned to the president and suggested, "Let's look at this list critically to see if there is anything we can do without or if there is anything we may have left off." After a thoughtful discussion of the necessary functions and contributions of a project manager, the consultants then gave their description of a successful project, in terms of project milestones, completion date, deliverables, system capabilities, and how and when it would start to produce cost-saving results—the Verifiable Benefits. They then asked a question to confirm the Felt Benefit: "If we can deliver what we've just outlined, would you be satisfied with the project?"

The consultants had decided to skip the step in the "What If" presentation model confirming that the prospect has the funds and authority to make the purchase because they knew that either the president had discretionary funds or would know how to get them. If it had turned out that they were wrong—that the president had no means to fund the project—the question of funding would have required a whole separate problem-solving session or negotiation.

The consultants went back to their "strawman," which now became their solution or offering, adding names of those who would work on the project and milestone dates. They explained how certain segments of the project would take more time than others and worked out a billing procedure that helped the college's cash flow. They asked the last question, "We can begin the project by the first of the month, would you like to give us the assignment?

With an affirmative answer from the president, the consultant agreed to draft[1] an engagement letter that included the price, billing agreement, and an outline of the work plan.

## CONCLUSION

A "what if" presentation—well conceived and orchestrated— often turns into a sale. It's important, however, that you go into such a presentation not expecting it to turn into a sale because if you have planned it as a subterfuge, you will not be effective in drawing out the opinions of your prospect and working with him or her to come up with something acceptable to both of you.

---

[1]Do not succumb to the temptation of bringing an engagement letter with you "just on the chance" that your prospect might agree with your "what if" proposal.

# 14

# WRITING AND DELIVERING YOUR PROPOSAL

When you get to this point in the sale, in most cases, there is little more that you can do to win the engagement. Now you must be sure that you don't lose it. As stated before, a good proposal can't overcome a bad job of selling, but a bad proposal can damage a good job of selling.

## THE FUNCTION OF THE PROPOSAL

Ideally, the proposal confirms in writing what you have already sold in person: Ideally, your buyer will skim through your proposal, grunting positively in the process, and then announce: "Yeah, that's everything we agreed to, let's get started." However, since sales conditions are seldom ideal, proposals must often do more than just confirm. For example, if there are members of the buying center whom you haven't met, your proposal must sell those people for you. And, for those of you who do

165

public sector work, where buyers hold sellers at arm's length, your proposal is often the primary selling device.

A proposal, no matter how beautifully written, is produced in a lean medium—the written word. That means it probably will not be carefully read, you will have no opportunity to get feedback and respond to it, you can't control the environment in which your proposal is read, and it cannot be changed: *It's your final statement.*

## DRAFT PROPOSAL OUTLINE

Because the proposal is such a weak sales device, you have to do everything you can to strengthen it. Especially if you have been unable to make a "what if" oral presentation, try to meet with your decision maker (or, at least, a key influencer) to go over an outline of your proposal draft. Bring your prospect a detailed outline and include any sentences or paragraphs that you expect may be controversial . . . to test for acceptability. Go through the outline carefully, asking for opinions.

Prepare questions in advance, such as:

Did I word this correctly?

Is this still valid?

Does this accurately summarize what we agreed to?

How is Tom going to react to this?

If you are meeting with the decision maker, let him or her, in essence, write your proposal for you.

In a sole-source situation, if you have done a good job on the outline, and if your decision-maker has voiced favorable opinions on it, you may be able to avoid writing the proposal altogether. Phil Tulley, a superb business developer in Australia, who at this writing is on the short side of 30, hasn't written a proposal in the past year; yet, he told me that he put around $450,000 of new business on the books last year. Tully has learned that if he does a solid job of selling and uses the draft proposal outline effectively, the decision maker will probably tell him to write an agreement or engagement letter and attach the corrected outline.

## WRITING A PROPOSAL

If you must write a proposal, make it something worth reading. And, please, do not begin your introduction with a brief but boring description of your prospect's company ("ABC, Inc. is a $1.6 million dollar manufacturing firm in the machine tools industry that employs 940 people") in the erroneous belief that such statements provide proof that you understand the client's business.

### Stress Benefits, Understate Features

In my experience, almost everyone who does any amount of selling claims to understand features and benefits: A feature is a noteworthy aspect of your offering or your capabilities, and benefits are the good things that features produce to fulfill your prospect's needs. In reading through scores of proposals for professional services, however, I have seen mostly features. Why is that? Maybe proposal writers expect their clients to know what benefits the features produce and, therefore, think the benefits are not worth mentioning.

For example, CPA firms have been known to state that they have a low partner-to-staff ratio, architects often say that the managing principal will provide continual oversight, consulting engineers sometimes promise that the project manager will devote, say, 80 percent of his or her time to the project. What are the benefits? Does the client really know? Or, do these features just sound like they must produce benefits?

A feature is a fact that the seller can state or describe. But, *benefit* is a relative term—something that *the buyer ultimately defines.* You can suggest a benefit, but the buyer must agree, or it's not a benefit. As a buyer, I may see no benefit in your being a full-service firm; I may see no benefit in your people doing a systematic survey of my needs; I may see no benefit in your experience in my industry. As a matter of fact, I may perceive every benefit you offer as a liability, not a benefit at all:

- Low partner-to-staff ratio may mean high billing rates.
- Continual oversight may mean that I am forced to talk to a person who thinks he or she knows what is going on rather than to the person who is actually doing the work.
- Being allotted 80 percent of the project manager's time sounds OK, as long as the 20 percent doesn't occur when I need him most.
- If you're experienced in my industry, you may not be able to take a fresh look at my needs.

Another good point to remember is that benefits cannot exist without needs. Every benefit—both verifiable and felt—should have been tested for validity before it appears in your proposal.

The preceding examples relate to second-order needs, that is, aspects of the services you will provide or the process involved in executing your work plan. (See Chapter 3.)

## Organizing Your Proposal

The Perfect Sales Equation tells you what content to include in your proposal. You pick the content sequence by evaluating how to present the information most effectively. Although the most conventional sequence starts with needs, I have seen excellent proposals that begin with the benefits, and I suppose a proposal could start with the offering or solution, but I have never seen one:

- *Section 1: Need(s).* Begin with a statement of the need as you understand it, followed by facts that verify it and the consequences making a solution urgent and important.
- *Section 2: Benefit(s).* Describe what success will look like— the desired future situation. If projected facts can verify the achievement of the desired future situation, include those facts.

- *Section 3: Offering/Solution.* Describe what you will do to achieve the desired future situation, highlighting your deliverables. Supplement that with your work plan or schedule. Describe your staffing by quantity and quality. In your work plan, cite the features you offer that will make your work plan effective (computer capabilities, experience of your people, techniques you have developed, etc.). If you have discovered second order needs, develop a subsection explaining how you can meet those service needs. If you are bidding on a Requirement, this section can produce your competitive advantage.

- *Section 4: Additional Information.* Include any information that substantiates your ability to do what you say you can do such as brief firm history, references, biographies of project team members.

## Writing Techniques

The best technique is—whenever possible—avoid writing proposals. The more you put on paper, other than contractual conditions, the more likely you are to say something with which your prospect will disagree. Engagement letters are much better because they are shorter, more general, and indicate a trusting relationship. But, if you must write a proposal, the following pointers will be helpful.

**Avoid Long Proposals.** Try to keep proposals under 10 pages. I was surprised by the results of an informal survey I made asking recipients of proposals how much time they spent reading them. Few people said they spent more than five minutes. They scanned sections on the deliverables and work plan and looked carefully at the pricing section. My guess is that the longer the proposal, the less time people will spend in reading it. When a 30-page document shows up in your in-basket, how do you deal with it (especially if you will *not* be held accountable for the information in that document)?

I have seen successful proposals that are nothing more than detailed topic outlines. I have seen successful proposals that are really engagement letters, supported by addenda. Don't feel compelled to write a massive proposal because that is what you have always done or because that is what you think your competition will do. Think about the readers, and write something that will meet *their* needs. As a general rule, the person who is most interested in your proposal is you. In today's world, when the acknowledged most powerful mass medium is the 20-second TV spot, don't expect fervent readers to intellectually devour your proposal.

**Avoid Executive Summaries.**   Such summaries tell readers that they don't need to read the rest of the proposal—the summary contains all the good stuff. If your proposal is so long that you need an executive summary, try to shorten your proposal. Executive summaries came into fashion and were useful when the quality of proposals was determined by their weight. However, if you have written a concise, well-organized short (6 to 10 pages) proposal, why add an executive summary and give someone an excuse not to read your proposal? If you must write a long proposal, put all the details into addenda. Include a table of contents so that people can find the detail they need to read.

**Write the Proposal Yourself.**   Someone junior to you who has never met the prospect and knows only what you have divulged about the project cannot produce a quality proposal. If you delegate, the writer will probably pull something off the computer, trying to make paragraphs from past proposals fit, and you'll end up with a generic proposal.

**Leave Out the Contract.**   Do not include a legal contract in a proposal or in a proposal addendum. They generally scare prospects half to death. Get the job, and then bring out the contract.

**Keep It Simple.**   Although everyone intuitively believes that his or her writing is comprehensible enough for an intelligent reader, a common complaint among literate business leaders is that almost no one knows how to write anymore (especially people coming out of graduate business schools). If you think you are a good writer, ask for comments from someone who frequently has to read what you write.

Find a good editor who can help you keep your writing simple. If you think you need more help or can't find a good editor, sign up for a writing seminar. Or study a book or two, such as Linda Flower's *Problem Solving Strategies for Writing*[1] or Richard A. Lanham's *Revising Business Prose.*[2]

**Provide Visual Interest.** Don't fill your proposal pages with single-spaced type. Companies in the *business* of communicating (newspapers, magazines, books) print their material in columns or short-measure lines that look more attractive and are easier to read. So, use a short-measure line and add extra space between lines. If you can include color in your charts and graphs, do it.

**Creativity—The RFP Dilemma.** Requests for proposals often produce dilemmas in that you feel compelled to respond in the requested manner, but you believe that you can represent your approach better creating your own strategy. Appendix A deals with this subject in detail.

## DELIVERING YOUR PROPOSAL

You must have some real good reasons to justify *not* making a proposal presentation. The best I can think of is that you really do not want the job. Or, the cost of a plane ticket exceeds your expected profit. If you *do* want the job, present your proposal.

Ideally, you will present your proposal with a colleague. You need another pair of eyes and ears to help you respond correctly to the difficulty and importance of this event. Try to have this person record all the questions that are asked so that later you can identify where your presentation may have lacked substance or clarity.

[1]Flower, Linda. 1981. New York: Harcourt Brace Jovanovich, Inc.
[2]Lanham, Richard A. 1981. New York: Charles Scribner's Sons.

## Hide the Book

When presenting the proposal content, do not hand out the proposal. Don't hand out the proposal even if you are presenting across the desk to one person who is your best friend. A proposal is a written document designed to serve as a written reference. It does not serve well as a presentation aid. If you distribute the proposal before your presentation, you give your audience the license to leaf through it while you are talking and to ask questions at will about anything it contains.

Develop slides, charts, or handouts specifically for presenting your proposal. Guide the presentation with an agenda or discussion outline. At the end of your presentation, ask if your proposal contains everything discussed and agreed to in previous meetings. If so, ask for the business.

## CLOSING

With the exception of short-list presentations, the objective of your presentation is to get acceptance of your proposal, to close. In the short-list presentation, since you can't close, your objective is to satisfy the prospect's selection criteria. If you can close, avoid cliché closes such as, "Would it be better if we started next Tuesday or next Thursday?" Be straightforward. Ask, "Do we have the business?" "May we begin work immediately?" or "Do you accept our proposal?"

If your decision maker cannot give you a definitive answer, ask what aspects of your proposal are still in question. Then, take any necessary steps to amend your proposal.

## FOLLOW-UP

If the decision maker cannot give you a conclusive answer, you need to plan some follow-up activity. The most common and useless follow-up is calling the prospect to ask if he or she has made a decision yet or if there is anything else you can do. Because the answer to both questions is no, why ask?

Instead, after your presentation, meet with your presentation team and debrief. Try to analyze where your proposal may be vulnerable. Take clues from the questions your audience asked and the issues you needed to explain or clarify. Try to talk to members of the Buying Center to get their opinions on the vulnerable aspects of your proposal. Then, at best, arrange a meeting with the decision maker or key influencers to amend or augment your proposal. As a minimum, write a letter to each Buying Center member to "set the record straight" or to "amplify a point of expressed interest." Where the decision seems to be taking an inordinately long time, send more information that expands or substantiates key points in your proposal. It can't hurt.

## COPING WITH FAILURE

You should convert better than 50 percent of your proposals: A realistic target is 75 percent. So, even if your hit rate is high, you will meet failure and you must learn to cope with it. I find transfer of aggression to be an effective means of coping. Blame everyone you can first—stupid clients, inept colleagues, wired political situations, competitors who bought the business. Once that is out of your system, review your Sales Probability Index and the Perfect Sales Equation and try to figure out where you were weak. Don't automatically blame your proposal or your proposal presentation. Analyze your sales effort before the proposal because that's where most sales are lost.

If you decide to call your prospect to find out why you lost or why someone else won, start the conversation by saying, "I'm not going to try to tell you made a bad decision or give you another explanation of why we really were the best. I just want to thank you for the opportunity and to learn from this experience." Then listen, clarify, paraphrase—and learn.

And, get after the next one.

# APPENDIX A

# REQUESTS FOR PROPOSAL, SHORT-LIST PRESENTATIONS, AND OTHER NIGHTMARES

When a Request for Proposal (RFP) arrives from an existing client, you have good reason to feel dismay: "Why are they going out for bid?" You expected a sole-source opportunity. When a RFP arrives from a company you've never done work for, you feel elated: "They must have problems with their existing relationships, and they must have heard good things about us." Both reactions are probably wrong. Paradoxically, more companies seem to be putting work out for competitive bid now than in the past, probably because of economic pressures. It is paradoxical, however, because this is supposed to be the age of "partnering" and of interactive communication, neither of which are consistent with the RFP process. Regardless of your reaction to the receipt of a RFP, you must find out why you received it. Is your client dissatisfied with your relationship? Why did the company select you as a candidate? As this subject unfolds, you will find that those are only two of a long list of questions you need answered after receiving a RFP.

## PURPOSE OF RFPs

None of the purposes that RFPs are supposed to serve has much effectiveness in enabling the purchaser to make the best buy. The avowed purpose is to provide sufficient information from which a qualified service provider can make a thoughtful proposal. The other, unstated purposes are to:

- Create the illusion that the proposal process provides a "level playing field."
- To save time; to avoid having to make people available to describe the project and to answer questions.

### Sufficient Information?

Most clients know that the RFP does not provide sufficient information, so they try to channel information through auxiliary means that don't function very well either. The Bidders' Conference invites all interested parties to attend a joint Question-and-Answer session. Bidders are selective about the questions they ask because they don't want to share important answers with their competitors. So, they ask innocuous questions and hope to get access to client personnel privately sometime in the future when they can put the really important questions. In anticipation of that maneuver, however, client personnel are usually instructed not to answer such questions because "they had ample opportunity to ask questions at the Bidders' Conference."

Another ineffective means for providing sufficient information is for a firm to instruct all bidders that they may submit their questions in writing, adding that in the interest of fairness to all parties, the firm will distribute answers to all competitors. Guess what kinds of questions are asked.

Best of all, but still not very good, some clients designate a person who will be available for questions. Unfortunately, that person is usually not very high level or well informed.

### Level Playing Field?

Most level playing fields exist only in myth. Great advantage goes to those who have done successful work in the past or who have been forewarned of the RFP and have taken the opportunity to do pre-RFP selling. The level playing field allows the advantaged to maintain their advantage and prohibits the disadvantaged from catching up. When you scrape away the cliché, neither the *illusion* of a level playing field nor a *genuinely* level playing field helps the client or the bidders. I'll try to justify this assertion shortly.

### To Save Time?

Many clients think it is unnecessary to spend time clarifying their RFPs. I have yet to talk to a client who admits that its RFP was confusing or incomplete. They say things like, "You may have to dig a little, but, if you read it carefully, I think you'll find everything you need is all there." Those of us who receive RFPs tend to disagree.

## BENDING THE RULES

Because you have probably experienced all the preceding frustrating barriers, you may wonder why I feel it necessary to mention them. I do so to remind you how counterproductive they are and to encourage you to find ways to circumvent them.

  If you are sneaky or brazen and break the rules, you will probably get caught and be disqualified. On the other hand, if you bend them by getting information from existing contacts or by persuading new contacts, you can probably ask forgiveness. For example, if you have access to the senior person involved with the RFP (presuming you are not dealing with purchasing agents), you can try to get permission to bend the rules. I have had some success with following approach:

- Tell your high-level contact that his firm and your firm share mutual self-interests: to produce a proposal that exactly meets the prospect's needs. If you submit a proposal that only partially meets the prospect's needs, it provides little value to the prospect and none to you. If all the competitive proposals only partially meet the prospect's needs, the choice will go to the one that comes closest—but that one will still miss. If you must rely on the RFP as your only source of information, your proposal will contain some guesses; you have to hope that you'll get lucky and your guesses will exactly meet the prospect's needs. On the other hand, if you can gain access to some key people, your chances of exactly meeting the prospect's needs will improve dramatically.

Although the logic is impeccable, it doesn't always work. But try it.

- If your contact says that giving you access would be unfair to the others, your answer is that it would be unfair only if your competitors also asked for access to key people and were refused. "If they have not asked," you can say with convincing sincerity, "it is probably because that they don't need more information or feel comfortable guessing."
- Another likely objection is, "We can't tie up our people answering questions." In response to this concern, you must tell your contact how many people you need to see and how much time it would take. The numbers are probably far less than the person had imagined. Then, presuming that the job itself carries a large price tag and importance to the organization, you can equate the amount of time you need as a reasonable investment to assure your prospect gets the best proposal possible: "I'm asking your organization to spend an extra 10 hours so that we can give you a proposal that will meet your needs. Because we are looking at a $250,000 assignment, that seems to be a reasonable investment."

This approach will work only with senior people who have the unilateral authority to open up communication. Don't expect a lower level person to try to sell this to his or her boss. If a senior person rejects your logic, the job is probably "wired" for one of your competitors. As a general rule, if your prospect insists on keeping you at arm's length, you should consider withdrawing from the competition.

**RESPONDING TO THE RFP**

The RFP will probably suggest some format, sequence, and content. Your proposal should respond in exactly the manner requested. Who knows how the proposal will be evaluated? In some instances, no one in the selection committee reads proposals until a short list has been compiled. And the short-list decisions may be made by people who evaluate by rigid criteria and fill in boxes on an assessment matrix. If a consultant was engaged to write the proposal, the consultant may also winnow the submissions into a short list. You certainly don't want your proposal thrown out because it did not follow the rules.

If you have some great ideas for alternative approaches, or changes in the scope, or anything else that makes sense to you and helps differentiate you from your competitors, package those suggestions in an addendum or a supplemental proposal. Be sure that your ideas are anchored by the Perfect Sales Equation. Seldom is an idea impressive enough that the buyer immediately recognizes the need it fills or the benefit it produces.

## SHORT-LIST PRESENTATION

Most professional service organizations have developed their own styles for short-list presentations, and many of them are just awful. The awful ones typically start with some senior executive of the firm, who tries to show the firm's commitment by introducing the firm and the presenters, and "setting the stage." The tenor of the speech makes it clear to everyone in the room that the person has done this same thing hundreds of times before, has had nothing to do with the proposal, knows very little about the job, and will play no role in getting the work done. (Senior executives can be extraordinarily effective in pledging the firm's commitment, but they must show the prospect that they understand the project and have accountability for performance.) Next, the project manager or account manager introduces a series of specialists who will explain the details (and the details and the details) of their special parts in the assignment. The manager then shows an organizational chart (your prospect has seen an equivalent from each competitor) showing his or her role as the liaison and communication link between the client and the consulting firm, and explains that his or her responsibility is to keep the project on track, on time, and on budget. A time line, or PERT chart, or Gantt chart, lays out the stages in the project and is followed by a brief glimpse at the budget and bottom line. There may be a few questions, and then the senior executive wraps things up with something inspirational.

### Competent? Credible? Compatible?

The conventional approach doesn't present many opportunities for the prospect to come to conclusions about your firm's competency, credibility, and compatibility. You can effectively break with convention, however, if you focus your presentation on what's special about this job, and what's special about your firm as related to the job. You can illustrate your competency by identifying critical aspects of the assignment that will require special expertise or experience, and then outline how you will deal with those difficulties. You can build credibility by pointing out unknown or difficult-to-predict job aspects and explaining how you will respond. You can show your compatibility by the tone of your presentation.

A colleague at a consulting engineering firm says the short-list presentation gives the buyer an opportunity to "kick the tires," to find out if you're the kind of people they want to work with. If you've been able to do some preproposal selling, you should know how they want to work with their consultants. I can think of a few kinds of relationships; maybe you can add to the list from your experience:

- *Take Charge People.* "You're the experts, you tell us."
- *Participative and Involving People.* "You're part of the family; let us know how we can help."
- *Careful and Sincere.* "No surprises; we want to be informed every step of the way."

You can create a presentation strategy that associates you with the relationship your prospect wants: powerful and direct; interactive; or low-key. Match your presentation style to the prospect's relationship needs. Glib, polished presenters can scare prospects who want consultants who are careful and sincere, and low-key presenters fail to impress prospects who are looking for a take-charge team of consultants.

### Short-List Objectives and Techniques

It does no good to ask for the assignment at the end of the short-list presentation because your decision maker cannot say yes at this time. Either more presentations must still be heard, or a competitive evaluation process must take place. Therefore, the objective for the short-list presentation is to find out if your proposal satisfies the prospect's selection criteria as well as the three universal criteria: competency, credibility, and compatibility.

Most presentations are put together at the last minute, and even if the presentation team does have the opportunity to rehearse, it's too late to make corrections. So, if you want to create a huge competitive advantage, prepare and rehearse. Most of your competitors won't.

You may be able to sell before the RFP is distributed, between the RFP and the proposal, and after the proposal. Although each approach presents problems, the best time to sell is before the RFP. As soon as your marketing intelligence detects that an RFP is coming,—even if it appears to be a long time in the future, start to call on the company and build relationships.

After the RFP has been distributed, it is very difficult to do any selling unless the prospect opens the organization to your questions or you have an established relationship that allows you to "call in some chips" for past favors. You can, however, do some selling after submitting your proposal. Try to contact key members of the selection committee and remind them that although you have tried to produce a proposal that exactly meets their needs, you would expect some misinterpretation or miscommunication. Then ask them if there were any areas where your proposal fell short or seemed confusing. They may give you something important that would allow you to submit an amendment. It's worth a try.

## SELLING TO TASK FORCES

A product of the 1990s spawned by concepts of empowerment, total quality management (TQM), and leadership, task forces now make purchasing decisions. In general, if you must sell to a task force, start looking somewhere else for business. There are so many dynamics going on in a given task force, it's almost impossible to predict how they will make the buying decision. A task force will usually make the most risk-free decision, but on the other hand, sometimes the members see defying the system as their mission in life.

Minimal-risk decisions are likely because many task force members are inexperienced and uncomfortable in making major decisions. Perhaps as task force membership becomes more commonplace, they will take greater risks. Task force members who take less ownership in its purpose and have less understanding of the issues, vote for the minimal risk when faced with a buying decision. Whereas senior people on task forces try to avoid influencing the group and, therefore, fall in line with a conservative decision. So, it is best not to propose something that requires courageous risk taking.

If you do accept the challenge of selling to a task force, try to identify the powers within the group. All task forces will have some leaders, and you need to spend time with them. Look for a consultant who may be working with the group, and then treat that consultant as an important member of the Buying Center. Try to meet with the group for a fact-finding session and insist on presenting your proposal personally to the group. If all your attempts fail and you are forced to sell at arm's length, you are probably in a competitive situation with low probability of success.

## Another Nightmare

The difficulties of selling to associations and, particularly, to the government are legend. Associations have so many buying influences and so many political intrigues that it is almost impossible to create a sales strategy. Selling to the government requires either political connections or a willingness to crank out proposal after proposal in the hope of converting a reasonable number. I have found the best way to get a good night's sleep is to concentrate my business on private sector corporations and let my competitors have the nightmares.

# APPENDIX B

# DEALING WITH PRICES

Professionals are notoriously poor at discussing the commercial aspect of their work: money. They have trouble discussing the price for the job, dealing with price objections, and negotiating price adjustments due to changes or corrections. As stated earlier in this book, the sooner you discuss prices, the more confident you will appear, the less likely your price will be challenged, and the more opportunity you will have to justify or negotiate. When you avoid or delay discussing prices, all kinds of bad things can happen.

## PRICE OBJECTIONS

Many consultants are vulnerable to price objections because they:

- Know their prices are negotiable.
- Believe that all price objections are real.
- Believe that the buyer knows competitive pricing.
- Dislike or avoid discussing prices.
- Focus on defending prices rather than on enhancing benefits.

Buyers of professional services soon recognize that they lose nothing by challenging your price. The challenge may be a legitimate concern stemming from a misunderstanding or disagreement with the value your service promises to provide. Or, it may be part of a game played to convince you to reduce your price. It's hard to detect which is which, but by knowing what might happen, you can better prepare yourself to respond appropriately to price objections.

If you understand where a buyer may be coming from, you will feel less defensive when your price is questioned. Unsophisticated, usually first-time, buyers of your service are likely to have legitimate concerns and misunderstandings about your price because of their inexperience and the risk they may feel when making the purchasing decision. Therefore, you should prepare yourself to detect and to respond to the following misunderstandings:

- The amount of time needed to perform a complex service.
- The legitimacy of "high" rates (they may compare your rates to their salaries).
- The specific deliverables.
- The verifiable benefits.

Sophisticated buyers who are experienced with consultants are more likely to play the following games to convince you to reduce your price:

- Tell you that they know your price is negotiable.
- Convince you that they know competitive prices.
- Allow you to believe your price is high.
- Tell you that the job is price sensitive and that they are likely to take the low bid.
- Give you a budget figure that they say is inflexible.
- Promise you opportunities for future business.

### Some Responses to Objections

**Your Price Is Negotiable.**  Prospects are playing hard ball when they tell you they know your price is negotiable. I have tried the following defenses:

Yes, on occasion we have negotiated prices. For example, when a client is under severe economic pressure, we may unbundle our services, or spread payments. If we find that we are far apart on price, it's usually because of some misunderstanding of the scope or the deliverables. And, of course, we'll renegotiate in that case. So, let's review the scope and the deliverables and the value that we think we can provide.

Yes, we have negotiated prices in the past, but more realistically, we have negotiated the assignment. We look at any assignment as having three areas of negotiation: price, scope, and timing. Some clients want the best price, the largest scope, and the work completed "yesterday." But that's unrealistic, and they know it, too. So, we are willing to give our clients any two out of the three. If you want the best price and the job completed right away, we have to reduce the scope; if you want a large scope and the job completed right away, you have to pay a premium price; if you want the best price and a large scope, you have to let us do the work on our choice of schedules. This approach injects some levity into the conversation while making some good points, and usually deflects the pricing challenge.

**Prospect Knows Competitive Prices.**  When your prospect tries to convince you that he or she knows competitive prices, you might respond: "I'm not surprised because we all work at much the same rate structure. The higher priced firms can command higher prices because of the quality and experience of their people, and systems that allow them to get the work out faster."

**Your Price Is High.**  If your customer tells you that your price is high, you must find out to what degree. If you are much higher than that desired by the prospect, you can say, "Undoubtedly we have some misunderstanding regarding the scope of work or deliverables." Take the opportunity to review both, and offer to restructure your price if you think it is necessary. If you are only slightly higher, shift the discussion to the Verifiable and Felt Benefits, and your commitment to deliver them.

**The Job Is Price Sensitive.**  Your prospect probably views your service as a commodity, and as long as that view remains intact he or she has little reason to buy other than the low price. To alter your prospect's opinion, educate the prospect or change the scope (if you can find verified needs), or review your pricing structure; it may be based on a 1980s marketplace.

**The Budget Is Inflexible.**    Listen carefully to your prospect, but figure that you can easily add 10 to 15 percent and stay within budget. I would believe a fixed budget figure only when given by a close friend in a long-term relationship, and then I would bet that he or she could get more money if I really justified it.

**There Are Opportunities for Future Business.**    "I can't promise anything, but I think there's a lot of future business here for your kinds of services; so I'd like you to sharpen your pencil on this one." Don't automatically count that as an insincere ploy to get you to cut price. Rather, take advantage of the opening and ask your prospect to share future plans with you. If the person can describe projected ideas without hesitancy and with conviction, anchoring them on something like a strategic plan or a vision statement, it might be worth giving a price break. Don't worry about adjusting your prices later, that's not hard to do unless you are quoting hours and rates, which I hope you don't.

## PRICE AND COMPETITIVE SELLING

If you think you might be the best qualified, but priced higher than your competitors, you should deal with that directly. If you can find out how much higher you are, present a justification of what the client will receive for the price difference. If you can't find out, end your proposal discussion with a statement such as this one:

> It's not unusual for us to be slightly higher than our competition because we attract and keep the highest quality people. If our price is a lot higher—and you are convinced that we are the best qualified for this job—I suspect there is some misunderstanding between us on the scope and deliverables of this job. If that's the case, I hope you will give us an opportunity to review our proposal carefully with you and see what adjustments can be made.

# APPENDIX C

# SELLING THE RESEARCH PHASE

Prospects often view the research phase of an engagement as a questionable expense. Intellectually, they understand its value, but they often resent having to pay for it and think they can shortcut the process by "filling you in" themselves or letting you interview a few "key people."

If you run into resistance getting funding for research, try this approach:

1. Specify the questions that you need to ask, and then ask your client if the answers to those questions are important to the project.
2. Ask if the information you seek is already available.
3. Specify whom you plan to query and ask (a) do they represent important groups of constituents, and (b) are you correct in thinking that their answers are likely to be different.

This strategy is consistent with the Perfect Sales Equation:

- *Verified Need.* We have insufficient information to plan a course of action.

- *Felt Need.* Proceeding without this information is likely to produce an invalid plan.
- *Verifiable Benefit.* The answers to these questions will give us the information we need to plan effectively.
- *Felt Benefit.* The plan we develop, based on this information, will have a high probability of success.
- *Offering/Solution.* Your research plan.

# APPENDIX D

# SELLING ADD-ON SERVICES AND FOLLOW-ON ENGAGEMENTS

The Business Development Process Model (see Chapter 2) indicates that discoveries you make while selling the initial or primary engagement (and although not diagramed, while doing the work) provide opportunities for add-on services and follow-on engagements. Often, these opportunities are blindly missed or clumsily muffed. David Maister points out, "First and foremost, it is most firms' experience that time spent marketing to existing clients is more likely to result in new business: existing clients represent *higher probability* prospects."[1] Please note that Maister did not say existing prospects are the easiest to sell.

## MISSED OPPORTUNITIES

In their zeal for efficiency, many professionals get in and out of clients' offices as quickly as possible, and rush back to the office to

[1]Maister, David H. 1989. "Marketing to Existing Clients." *Journal of Management Consulting,* 5(2): 5.

dive into the job. Consequently, they miss opportunities gained by hanging around and being available for someone to say, "Do you guys know anything about . . . ?" One of the best business developers I know convinced his client—a large insurance company—to assign him a spare office. People started thinking of him as "one of the family" and his business with that firm exploded.

## MUFFED OPPORTUNITIES

Because you can easily overestimate the closeness of your relationship and conceive yourself as "one of the family," you can also conclude that you don't need to sell. The buying decision, however, is the same whether you sell to a stranger or to a buddy: The offering has to fulfill a verified and felt need and produce a verifiable and felt benefit. The only reasons selling to an existing client may be easier than to a new prospect are that you probably have better access to the Buying Center and you have a track record.

The process for selling add-on and follow-on work is basically the same as the sequence described in Chapter 9. If you work the Perfect Sales Equation carefully, you probably have a 90 percent chance of getting a sole-source opportunity.

# APPENDIX E

# TEAM SELLING

The practice of team selling is becoming more and more common because, although expensive, it has proven very effective. However careful a listener one person may be, personal biases, attention span, and focused self-interests make it likely that he or she will misinterpret something a prospect says or miss an opening that leads to an opportunity for business. The downside of team selling is its execution.

Both parties need to plan the call and *agree on the intended outcome*, that is, what you want your prospect to give you: information, opinions, permission to proceed. If you represent different disciplines, you must assist each other in conducting directed interviews. You need to practice the art of not interrupting, but you must step in and help your partner clarify questions that have not been well answered or points that have been misunderstood.

# APPENDIX F

# PROMOTIONAL SEMINARS

One of the popular business development tactics of the 1980s was the promotional seminar. Brokers, bankers, and consultants of all sorts and sizes tried to drum up business by sponsoring seminars that they hoped would produce many qualified leads. Most seminar sponsors were disappointed with the results, and today the practice has all but died out. Can the death be attributed to a bad idea? Or, might it be a good idea with bad execution? I think the latter. Furthermore, enough time has passed for most people to have forgotten what a waste of time most seminars were. This creates an opportunity to use seminars as an effective business development tool.

## INVESTMENT EQUALS OPPORTUNITY

The simple solution to having a productive seminar is to invest enough care in the planning and execution to make it work. A valuable seminar can produce enormous business development opportunities. Therefore, it doesn't make sense to turn the planning over to juniors who don't have the resources to do it and the execution to seniors who will get up in front of important prospect and wing it.

## A SUGGESTED APPROACH

First, decide the seminar objective: Is it business development or is it advertising? Business development means you want to create leads, and advertising means you want to create awareness. For the former, you want a relatively small audience, for the latter you want a large one.

### Time Schedule and Content

The following schedule suggests the steps to take when planning a seminar. It is followed by an expanded outline with specific tips.

| Weeks to Seminar | Activity |
|---|---|
| 13 | Select potential topics |
| 12 | Form the seminar team |
| | • Select team members; set responsibilities |
| | • Develop objective and content |
| | • Confirm time commitments of team members |
| 10 | Plan the seminar |
| | • Time and facility |
| | • Number of attendees |
| | • Audience: level, industries, company size |
| 9 | Develop seminar content |
| | • Confirm topic, objective, audience |
| | • Plan delivery resources; begin checking presenter availabilities |
| | Plan the invitation |
| 8 | Select Resources |
| | • Confirm presenters' time commitments for planning, preparation, practice |
| | Plan follow-up activities |
| | • Postinvitation |
| | • Postseminar |
| 7 | Send invitations |
| 6 | Presenter Preparation |
| | • Review message concepts |
| | • Arrange for presentation aids |
| | • Plan rehearsal schedule |

| | |
|---|---|
| 3 | Invitation Follow-Up; confirm facility and arrangements |
| 1 | Dry Run |

## Seminar Tips

**Select Potential Topics (*S*-13).**[1]   The topics you choose must have *important* financial/legal/moral consequences to an organization. That is, if organizations do things right, they get rewarded; if they do things wrong, they get punished. Your seminar should be a start toward helping organizations to do things right or to avoid doing things wrong.

**Form the Seminar Team (*S*-12).**   Pick team members who have a direct, immediate, and important stake in the success of the seminar. They win if it is successful; they get hurt if it fails. Those who do not have a big stake in the success will lack commitment.

Let the seminar team develop a few topics, using the previously described criteria. Start thinking about seminar objectives. If your objective is advertising, that's easy. If it's business development, use the following thought process:

- *Objective.* At the end of the seminar, I want the attendees to *decide* that they have a *need* to take some *action now* and that they *need help* from my company.
- *Consider This Question.* What's the expected verified or felt need, what's the action they should take, why now, and what's the help you can offer?

Ensure that team members have blocked out time to work on the seminar. If they don't make it a priority on their schedules, more immediate pressures will take precedence.

**Plan the Seminar (*S*-10).**   Determine when in the day and in the week you want to hold the seminar, and how long it will be. The only definitely bad times in the week are Monday morning and Friday afternoon. Two hours is a minimal time for an important topic. Really important topics can merit a half-day session. Breakfast and luncheon

---

[1]*S:* Weeks to seminar.

meetings are good because they involve a "necessary" event, so people are inclined to attend. On the other hand, they add expense, consume time, and present distractions.

Your "feel" for the session will tell you the desired number of attendees. Small groups—10 to 12—make good group discussion more likely. Large groups tend to reinforce the importance of the topic but inhibit discussion. Large groups are more important if your objective is advertising.

If you decide to have a smaller group and desire good group interaction, think about the effects of attendees with dissimilar characteristics: different industries, job titles, and company sizes. Will the differences inhibit or contribute to good discussion? If they will inhibit, plan to group audiences according to industries, titles, or company sizes.

Choose two or three possible facilities for the seminar. Since you have not yet identified scope and character, you don't know what size room you will need so find one room for a group of 50, another for 25, another for 12. Book all options now and cancel later. The facility you select should be congruent with the character of your seminar.

**Develop Seminar Content (S-9).**    Think about the topic, the objective, the size, and the character of the group. Because these qualities are *interdependent*, what will work for a group, topic, or objective in one situation may not work in another.

Develop a list of potential presenters. Do you need "name" presenters, or will organizational affiliations be sufficient? Have you heard the potential presenters speak before? Do they have a *real* stake in the success? If you use outside speakers and don't pay them, can you control them? Will they commit time for preparation and rehearsal? Will they take direction from you, or will they want to "do their own thing"? Be sure you have backup presenters in case someone cancels at the last-minute *or* doesn't perform to your standards.

Begin to develop the strategy for presenting your content. Your objective drives your content strategy. Eliminate any content that does not move your audience toward your objective. Consider your objective as a *decision* you want the attendees to make at the end of your seminar. That decision involves a series of subdecisions leading to the final decision. Put yourself in the heads of the attendees. For them to decide to do what you want them to do, what subdecisions do they have to make? Once you have figured that out, you then know the content strategy of your presentation.

**Example**

*Topic and Premise.* Compensation and benefit practices that appeared appropriate in the late 1980s, if not changed, will probably seriously harm middle market companies in the 1990s.

*Objective.* At the end of the seminar, we want the invitees to decide that they need to take specific action *now* to avoid the predictable harm and that our firm can provide the means for avoiding that harm.

*Strategy.* What subdecisions will cause them to arrive at that final decision?

**Plan the Invitation (S-9).**   What is the usual ratio of invitees to attendees? No one knows. Pick a bad topic and send a bad invitation, and you won't get anyone. A good ratio to work with is 3:1. Because you have booked rooms of different sizes, you'll be able to adjust to the response. Include an RSVP return card with your invitation.

Keep the invitation simple, but get professional design help. If you want high-level people, make it elegant. State the *need* that your seminar addresses and stress what the need will *cost* the organization. Cite the *consequences of doing nothing,* or *doing the wrong thing.* Promise *direction* for resolving the need and cite the credentials of your presenters.

**Select Resources (S-8).**   When you ask people to be presenters, do not downplay the time commitment and be sure to reward the presenters for their work. Their degree of commitment will be commensurate with the value of their reward. This applies to both *internal* and *external* resources.

**Plan Follow-Up Activities (S-8).**   Someone needs to call the invitees to remind them of the invitation and to ask them to come. This person must be capable and prepared to *sell* the seminar over the phone. This is not a job for a junior secretary or intern. He or she must be fluent in the seminar topic, its importance, and the value that the seminar will provide. Work out a script for the follow-up telephone call (then don't let the person use it) and do role-play practice. The phone call *is more likely to sell* the seminar than the invitation.

Decide what you will do after the seminar. Who will follow up? How will they do that? What's the predictable next step in the selling process?

**Send Invitations (S-7).**    When is the "right" time to send an invitation? There isn't any; there are only good guesses. Seven weeks ahead allows the invitation to arrive when the invitee may be out of town and still have six-weeks advance notice.

**Presenter Preparation (S-6).**    Once you know your content strategy, then you know what you want your presenters to deliver. They should understand your strategy and *agree* to work within it. This is not the place for free-lance creativity. Don't expect this to come easily. Presenters are famous for agreeing with everything you say, procrastinating, and then, at the last minute, putting together a variation of something they have done in the past. Insist on seeing a presentation outline well in advance of the seminar; *don't compromise your strategy!*

Arrange for someone to help your presenters with presentation aids. Don't let them use 35-mm slides. Avoid overhead slides unless they have been professionally done. Flip charts are not acceptable with groups over 25. If you want handouts, be sure they all fit together visually and conceptually.

You must have an early rehearsal. Don't be kind to the presenters if they don't deserve it. If you will reward them for their performance, you have a right to insist on your standards of quality. Have backup presenters ready.

**Invitation Follow-Up (S-3).**    Be aware of how well the follow-up calls are going. You may have to bring in some well-known names to pump up attendance. Have a backup, big-gun plan ready. You do not want to hold a seminar for four people (and have 25 empty chairs). Nor do you want to cancel your seminar. Select your facility and confirm reservations and arrangements.

**Dry Run (S-1).**    Try to do it in the seminar facility, or a similar facility. Practice with all presentation aids. If you plan for your people who are not presenters to attend, be sure they know their roles. For example, if you have a program with a break in it (if longer than $1^1/2$ hours, you need a break), instruct them to "work" the crowd during the break and pick up information. As a rule, you can gather more good information during breaks than during question and answer periods. Then, use the information to guide the rest of your program.

## CONCLUSION

Seminars provide wonderful opportunities to showcase your think-ing, your capabilities, and your people. Some professional firms do a superb job of planning and executing their seminars and reap great benefits. Others try to wing it, promising the attendees far more than the seminar can deliver. Because such firms have fuzzy objectives, they have no cogent follow-up plan. The massive changes we can ex-pect in the 1990s will provide fertile material for professional semi-nars. If you treat seminars as major business development events, they will pay off handsomely.

# APPENDIX G

# BUILDING AND MAINTAINING RELATIONSHIPS

Business developers are often admonished by their management to *build relationships* and, then once they are built, to *maintain relationships*. The problem with those mandates is that everyone understands the words, but not everyone understands what to do. In building a relationship, friendship is not the goal, although it may become the by-product. The following is a model for building relationships:

- Identify the key players in your client organization: decision makers, users, and ratifiers. Assign members of your account team to specific people. Your executive-level people should focus on the ratifiers; you should focus on the decision makers; and your project specialists should focus on the users. If you're the whole team, you get all three.
- Plan the frequency of face-to-face contact; the telephone is not a good substitute. As a general rule, add 10 minutes to every client visit and use that time to see someone on your relationship list.
- Provide something of business value on most of your visits—some information or an idea that helps your client achieve goals. Don't

count on entertainment to build or maintain a relationship. While it helps, it is not a substitute for bringing something of value.

- Do good work.
- Demonstrate accountability: Show integrity by doing the right thing even when you must place your self-interests at risk.
- Manage conflict by dealing with it immediately and nondefensively.

In addition to relationship building activities, you need to have the following:

- *Work-in-Process Reviews.* Hold open discussions with key players from both parties on how things are going. Set up a regular schedule and stick to it.
- *Lessons-Learned Evaluations.* At the end of the project, review the outcomes and what both parties have learned so that the next project will go more smoothly.
- *Relationship Evaluations.* Set up executive-level discussions on how the relationship is progressing; or use an outside resource to interview key clients for annual or biannual evaluations.
- *Account Review.* Hold an annual meeting of project teams with their client counterparts to review what, together, you have accomplished. Produce reports that are distributed to both the teams and subject organizations.

Building and maintaining relationships does not happen by accident. What's more, because it is hard to put a short-term pay-outs on relationship activities, they are easily postponed in favor of short-term necessities. You must have discipline to build and maintain relationships or you will only create the illusion.

# INDEX

## S

Sales interviews
  case history of failed sales
    pitch, 14–15
  evaluation of, 16
  sidetracking of conversation as
    pitfall, 13–14
Sales Probability Index, 119–127,
  140–141
Scope of project, clarification of,
  140–141
Selling defined, 1–3
Seminars for promotional
  purposes, 193–199
Senge, Peter, 51
Services, selling of, 8–10
Short-list presentations, 179–181
Sole sourcing, 101, 112, 115,
  120, 130, 145, 166, 175, 190
Solicitation of business, 126,
  147, 152
  business functions, at, 80
  cold calls, *See* Cold calls
  social situations, in, 78–80
Solutions as sales strategy
  defined, 13
  identifying solutions, 18,
    20–21, 24–25
Straight re-buys, 112–114
Strategies
  development of, *See*
    Development of strategies
  solutions as, 13, 18, 20–21,
    24–25

## T

Task forces for buying, 134
  presentations to, 181–182
Team selling, 200
Telephone use as selling tool, 40,
  46, 84–86, 201
Time factors, 8–9
Tully, Phil, 166–167
Type of buy
  modified re-buys, 113–114
  new buys, 113–114
  straight re-buys, 112–114

## V

Verifiable benefits for client
  identification of, 99, 141
  importance of, 25–27
Verifiable benefits to client
  defined, 11–13, 15, 20
Verifiable needs of client
  defined, 11–13, 15
  identification of, 23–24,
    70–72, 91, 148–149
  Information gathering to
    determine, 19–21, 70–72

## W

Webster, Frederick E., 103
Wind, Yoram, 103, 112